Third
Edition

Grade **5**

FINISH LINE

MATHEMATICS

Continental

CREDITS

Photos: United States coin images from the United States Mint

ISBN 978-0-8454-7887-5

TABLE OF CONTENTS

About Finish Line Mathematics

Finish Line Mathematics, Third Edition, will help you prepare for math tests. Each year in math class, you learn new skills and ideas. You build on the math skills you already have; you prepare to learn new math skills in the future. As your mathematics knowledge grows, it is important to master the concepts you learn each year. Then you will better understand the ideas you will learn next year.

This book is divided into units of related lessons. Each lesson concentrates on one main math idea. The lesson reviews things you have learned in math class. Each lesson is broken into four parts.

Introduction

The Introduction of each lesson reviews the math skill. It provides explanations and examples. It reviews important math vocabulary. You may see pictures and diagrams to help you understand the skill.

Focused Instruction

The Focused Instruction part guides you through two or more practice problems. First, you will read the problem. Then you will work through a series of questions to help you find the answer. Sometimes the instructions will ask you to work with a partner. As you work through the problem, you will practice the skills you need to understand the main idea of the lesson. There are hints and reminders along the sides of the pages to help you remember what you have learned. At the end of the Focused Instruction, you will do one to three additional problems; these problems do not have hints.

Guided Practice

The third part is Guided Practice, where you will work alone to complete two to three problems. These problems are open-ended, which means you have to write the answer. You may have to show your work, make a graph, draw a diagram, or do some other mathematical task. Again, there will be hints and reminders to help you out.

(4) Independent Practice

Finally, you will complete the Independent Practice. You will work by yourself to complete two to three pages of questions. These questions will be a variety of item types. In addition to multiple-choice and open-ended questions, you will also do multiple-choice items with more than one correct answer. You may need to fill in a table with information or complete a sentence or equation. Always look carefully at the question to decide the correct way to answer it. You may not be familiar with all the question types. Ask questions if you do not understand. The Independent Practice does not have any hints or reminders. You must use everything you learned in the first three parts to complete this section.

At the end of each unit is a unit review. In the review, you will use all the skills you worked on in that unit. You will see different item types, just like in the Independent Practice section. There will not be any hints or reminders.

A glossary and a set of flash cards appear at the end of the book. The glossary contains important words and terms along with their definitions from the book. The flash cards will help you review important ideas, formulas, and symbols from the book. There are some blank flash cards, too. You can use these to make flash cards for the things you most need to work on.

Developing your math skills will help you as you continue to learn and will allow you to use math in your everyday life.

Big Ideas from Grade 4

In grade 4, you learned some of the properties for addition, subtraction, multiplication, and division, and how to apply these skills in word problems. You also learned how to compare fractions and new ways to measure area. Now, you can use these skills to solve word problems, learn new systems of measurement, and work with more complex sets of numbers and fractions.

LESSON 1 Multiplying and Dividing Whole Numbers In this lesson, you will multiply and divide whole numbers.

LESSON 2 Understanding Decimals In this lesson, you will use the base ten system, place-value charts, and number lines to work with decimal numbers.

LESSON 3 Adding and Subtracting Fractions In this lesson, you will add and subtract fractions and use fraction models.

LESSON 4 Finding Equivalent Measurements In this lesson, you will calculate equivalent measurements within both customary and metric systems of measurement.

 Introduction

Multiplication is a way to show repeated addition of the same number. The numbers that you multiply are **factors,** and the answer you find is the **product.**

One method of multiplying is by making an **area model,** which is a rectangular model divided into squares.

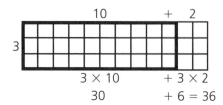

The area model has 3 rows of 12 squares for a total of 36 squares. You can write $3 \times 12 = 36$.

For larger numbers, you can use vertical multiplication. Vertical multiplication is a shortened version of multiplying by place value.

$$
\begin{array}{r}
24 \\
\times 11 \\
\hline
24 \\
+240 \\
\hline
264
\end{array}
$$

Write the numbers by aligning the digits in the same place. Then multiply one place value at a time and add the partial products.

Division separates a number into equal groups. Multiplication and division are **inverse operations,** or operations that "undo" one another. To divide small numbers, you can use mental math or fact families. For greater numbers, you can use long division.

Find the quotient of $371 \div 7$.

$$
\begin{array}{r}
53 \\
7\overline{)371} \\
-35\downarrow \\
\hline
21 \\
-21 \\
\hline
0
\end{array}
$$

Start with the hundreds place. Check if 7 goes into 3. It does not.
Move to the next place. Check if 7 goes into 36. It does, about 5 times.
Subtract the product of 5 and 7, 35, from 37.
Bring down the next number from the dividend, 1.

Check if 7 goes into 21. It does, 3 times.
Subtract the product of 3 and 7, 21, from 21.

There are no more numbers to bring down. So $371 \div 7 = 53$.

Think About It

A three-digit number is multiplied by a one-digit number. How can you check that the results are correct without the use of a calculator?

_____

_____

_____

② Focused Instruction

Use multiplication and division to solve word problems.

➤ Thomas took a bicycle trip through Montana. He rode a total of 378 miles in 9 days. If he rode approximately the same number of miles each day, what were his average miles per day?

Is the problem asking for a greater or lesser value than the total number of

miles? _____

What operation is needed to find the average miles per day?

_____

Divide the total number of miles by the number of days.

Can 3 be divided by 9? _____

Can 37 be divided by 9? _____ If so, how

many times? _____

Complete the problem in the space at the right.

What is the average number of miles per day? _____

What operation can be used to check your
work? _____

Use the space below to verify the reasonableness of your answer.

> What is the inverse operation of division?

Think about the place value of each digit as you multiply.

➤ Multiply 14 × 42.

What digit is in the ones place of 14? _____

What digit is in the ones place of 42? _____

What is the product of the ones in the two factors? _____

What digit is in the tens place of 42? _____

What is the value of the tens place of 42? _____

What is the product of the tens in 42 and the ones in 14? _____

What is the value of the tens place of 14? _____

What is the product of the tens in 14 and the ones in 42? _____

What is the product of the tens in both factors? _____

What is the sum of all the partial products? _____

Find the product using vertical multiplication.

$$\begin{array}{r} 42 \\ \times 14 \\ \hline \end{array}$$

> Remember that the product of the multiplication problem is the sum of the partial products.

Use what you know about multiplication and division to solve these problems.

1 432 ÷ 8 = _____

2 17 × 59 = _____

3 814 ÷ 11 = _____

4 23 × 22 = _____

Solve the following problems.

1 A dance contest gives each dancer 45 seconds to compete. In all, there are 72 dancers competing. For how many total seconds are dancers allowed to compete? Solve the problem in two different ways. Show your work.

> Remember to use a 0 as a placeholder in the second partial product.

Answer _____ seconds

2 For a school party, the cafeteria workers make 2,712 ounces of lemonade. They fill cups for students to drink during the party. If each cup holds 8 ounces of lemonade, how many cups can the workers fill? Show your work.

> Think of the operation that is used to separate into smaller units.

Answer _____ cups

3 Find the product of 15 × 18.

> Use vertical multiplication.

Answer _____

Solve the following problems.

1 A coach's swimming team practices 5 times per week. There are 4 age groups on the team, and each group practices at a different time. Each group practices a total of 60 minutes per practice. What is the total amount of time the coach spends at practice during the week?

   A   240 minutes

   B   300 minutes

   C   540 minutes

   D   1,200 minutes

2 An online movie rental company charges $18 per month to watch up to 20 movies during that month. Milly can pay the fee of $18 per month or a 6-month fee of $102 for the same number of movies per month.

   Part A Which choice will cost Milly less over a 6-month period?

   Answer _____

   Part B Explain how you found your answer.

   _____

   _____

   _____

3 Hank is buying new curtains for his house. Each window will need 2 curtain panels to cover it. He has a total of 16 windows in his house. The curtain panels that he plans on buying are $29 each. He determines that he will spend a total of $203 on curtains using the multiplication below.

$$
\begin{array}{r}
5 \\
29 \\
\times 16 \\
\hline
174 \\
+29 \\
\hline
203
\end{array}
$$

Part A Hank made two mistakes, a calculation error and a missed step. What errors did Hank make in his multiplication?

_____

_____

Part B What is the total amount Hank will spend on curtains? Show your work.

Answer $_____

4 An art supply store allows customers to fill a box with 8 colored pencils for $3. They have a total of 696 colored pencils in stock. Each box of colored pencils costs the store $1 to buy from the pencil factory. How much money will the art supply store make, after paying the pencil company, if they sell all of the pencils in boxes of 8 pencils? Show your work.

Answer $_____

5 Terrance is putting away holiday decorations. He has 204 ornaments that need to be put away into plastic containers. Each container has 6 sections, and each section can fit 1 ornament. How many plastic containers will Terrance fill putting away his ornaments?

Answer _____ plastic containers

6 A printer can print sheets of labels like the one shown below.

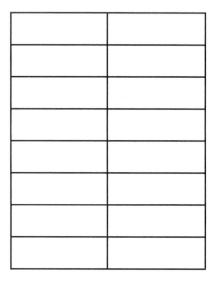

Part A If a package of label sheets contains 18 sheets, how many labels are in each package?

Answer _____ labels

Part B Another sheet has larger labels. There are 2 times as many labels on the sheet above as on the sheet with larger labels. If the number of sheets in a package of larger labels remains the same, how many larger labels are in a package?

Answer _____ labels

1 Introduction

Recall that our number system is a base ten system. The value of the next greatest place is 10 times the value of the place before. The value of the next lowest place is $\frac{1}{10}$ the value of the place after. **Decimals** follow the same place-value pattern as whole numbers.

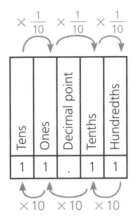

Each place value increases or decreases by a factor of 10.

A fraction written with a denominator of 10 or 100 can be written as a decimal using the denominator to describe the place value. Look at the denominator of the fraction. Count the zeros. Place the decimal point the same number of places to the right.

$$\frac{4}{10} = 0.4 \qquad \frac{45}{100} = 0.45$$

To compare the two decimals, look at the values of each place. Both decimals have 4 tenths, but the second decimal also has 5 hundredths, while the first decimal does not have any hundredths. The second decimal, 0.45, is greater than the first decimal, 0.4: $0.45 > 0.4$.

You can use a 0 as a placeholder without changing the value.
$0.4 = .4 = 0.40$

Decimals can be located and compared on a number line.

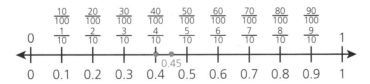

Notice that 0.4, or $\frac{4}{10}$, is less than 0.45, or $\frac{45}{100}$, because 0.4 is farther to the left on the number line than 0.45.

The decimal 0.4 can be written as $\frac{4}{10}$, 0.40, and $\frac{40}{100}$.

Think About It

Explain why the numbers 0.70, 0.7, $\frac{70}{100}$, and $\frac{7}{10}$ all represent the same value.

_____

_____

_____

_____

2 Focused Instruction

Use a number line or grid to help write or compare decimals. Answer the questions that follow.

➤ Write $\frac{56}{100}$ and $\frac{6}{10}$ as decimals and compare.

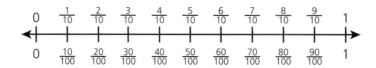

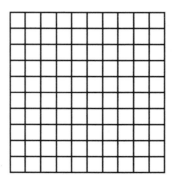

Write $\frac{56}{100}$ in words. _____

Write $\frac{6}{10}$ in words. _____

To write $\frac{56}{100}$ as a decimal, in which place should the 5 be

written? _____ The 6? _____

To write $\frac{6}{10}$ as a decimal, in which place should the 6 be written? _____

What is the decimal equivalent of $\frac{56}{100}$? _____

What is the decimal equivalent of $\frac{6}{10}$? _____

Compare the two decimals using a comparison symbol.

_____ ◯ _____

> Use these symbols to compare numbers:
> - is greater than (>)
> - is less than (<)
> - is equal to (=)

➤ What values belong in the boxes on the number line below?

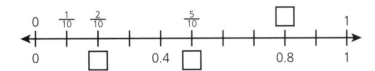

What does the denominator of the fraction equivalent of the first and second missing numbers mean? _____

What is the numerator of the fraction that is equivalent to the first missing number? _____ What is the first missing number? _____

What is the numerator of the fraction that is equivalent to the second missing number? _____ What is the second missing number? _____

What is the place value of the 8 in the third number? _____

How does the place value of the decimal determine the denominator of the fraction equivalent?

_____

What is the third missing number? _____

Complete the comparison statements by placing a comparison symbol in each circle.

1 0.82 $\bigcirc$ $\frac{8}{10}$

2 0.06 $\bigcirc$ $\frac{6}{10}$ $\bigcirc$ $\frac{65}{100}$

3 $\frac{4}{10}$ $\bigcirc$ 0.39 $\bigcirc$ $\frac{4}{100}$

Solve the following problems.

1 The average lengths of three different types of ants are shown in the table below.

ANT LENGTHS

Type of Ant	Average Length (in inches)
Fire Ant	$\frac{25}{100}$
House Ant	0.12
Carpenter Ant	$\frac{5}{10}$

> Write each of the numbers in the same form before comparing.

Which ant has the greatest average length, in inches?

Answer _____

2 Look at the comparison below.

$$\frac{3}{10} = 0.03$$

> The denominator of the fraction also describes the place value of the 3 in decimal form.

Part A Is the comparison statement correct? Explain why or why not.

_____

_____

Part B Use the grids below to prove your answer to Part A is true.

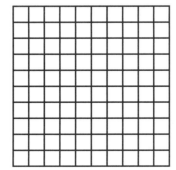 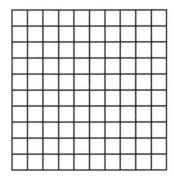

Solve the following problems.

1 Which list shows equivalent fractions and decimals? Select the **two** correct answers.

A 0.50, $\frac{5}{100}$, $\frac{50}{100}$

B $\frac{5}{10}$, $\frac{50}{100}$, 0.05

C 0.50, $\frac{5}{10}$, $\frac{50}{100}$

D $\frac{5}{100}$, $\frac{50}{10}$, 0.05

E 5.0, $\frac{50}{10}$, $\frac{500}{10}$

F 0.50, $\frac{50}{100}$, 0.5

2 What fraction, with a denominator of 10, is equivalent to 0.80?

Answer _____

3 The Galapagos tortoise moves at a speed of $\frac{3}{10}$ kilometer per hour. The three-toed sloth moves at a speed of 0.24 kilometer per hour. Which animal has a greater speed? Explain how you found your answer.

_____

_____

_____

4 A slice of bread weighs about 0.02 kilogram. What is the weight of the bread slice written as a fraction?

A $\frac{2}{10}$ kilogram

B $\frac{20}{10}$ kilogram

C $\frac{2}{100}$ kilogram

D $\frac{20}{100}$ kilogram

5 Explain how to write the decimal 0.97 as a fraction.

_____

_____

6 Gwen made a poster for a science project. Gwen's poster measured $\frac{76}{100}$ meter tall and $\frac{35}{100}$ meter wide. What is the decimal notation for each fraction? Find and mark the decimals on the number line below.

0   0.1   0.2   0.3   0.4   0.5   0.6   0.7   0.8   0.9   1
meter   . meter

7 Kano has the coins shown below in his pocket.

Part A Write the values of each coin as a decimal.

Penny _____

Dime _____

Quarter _____

Part B Write the value of each coin as a fraction with a denominator of 100.

Penny _____

Dime _____

Quarter _____

Part C Kano finds another coin worth $\frac{5}{100}$ dollar on the ground and puts it in his pocket. What coin did Kano find on the ground?

Answer _____

LESSON

3 Adding and Subtracting Fractions

① Introduction

A fraction can be used to describe the number of equal parts in a whole. A fraction describes $\frac{parts}{whole}$, where the **numerator** is the number of parts being talked about and the **denominator** is the total number of parts in the whole.

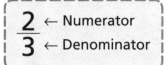

$\dfrac{2}{3}$ ← Numerator
← Denominator

You can add fractions together much like you do whole numbers. The model below shows the sum of $\frac{1}{3} + \frac{1}{3}$. Notice that the denominators are the same.

$$\frac{1}{3} \quad + \quad \frac{1}{3} \quad = \quad \frac{2}{3}$$

When adding fractions with the same denominator, you add the numerators. Keep the denominator the same. The same is true for subtraction. If the denominators are the same, subtract the numerators and keep the denominator the same.

Some fraction problems may involve a **mixed number,** which has a whole number part and a fraction part. There are two ways to add or subtract mixed numbers. One way is to add or subtract the whole number parts and the fraction parts separately.

Add $2\frac{3}{8} + 1\frac{4}{8}$.

Find the sum of the whole numbers. Then, find the sum of the fractions.

$$2 + 1 = 3 \qquad\qquad \frac{3}{8} + \frac{4}{8} = \frac{7}{8}$$

$$3\frac{7}{8}$$

Another way is to rewrite each mixed number as an **improper fraction.** To write an improper fraction, multiply the denominator by the whole number and add the original numerator to find the numerator of the improper fraction. Use the same denominator.

> An improper fraction has a numerator that is greater than its denominator.
> $\frac{6}{4}$

A trail mix recipe calls for $2\frac{5}{8}$ cups of cereal and $\frac{7}{8}$ cup of raisins. How many cups of trail mix will there be in all?

You can rewrite as $2\frac{5}{8}$ as $\frac{21}{8}$. Add. Then simplify the result.

$$\frac{21}{8} + \frac{7}{8} = \frac{28}{8}$$
$$= 3\frac{4}{8}$$
$$= 3\frac{1}{2}$$

There are $3\frac{1}{2}$ cups in all.

> To change an improper fraction to a mixed number, divide the numerator by the denominator. The quotient is the whole number. The remainder is the numerator of the fraction. The denominator stays the same.
>
> $$28 \div 8 = 3 \text{ R}4 = 3\frac{4}{8}$$

Think About It

Explain how to find the difference of a mixed number and an improper fraction. Give an example to prove your reasoning.

_____

_____

_____

2 Focused Instruction

Add and subtract fractions to solve problems.

➤ A cup contains $2\frac{1}{3}$ ounces of water. A second cup contains $3\frac{1}{3}$ ounces of water. Find the total amount of water in both cups.

What is the sum of the whole numbers? _____

Which part of the fraction, the numerator or the denominator, do you add? _____

What is the sum of the fractions? _____

What is the total amount of water in both cups?

_____

> The numerator is the number of parts being talked about. The denominator is the total number of parts.

➤ Matteo is wrapping a present. He needs $\frac{5}{8}$ yard of ribbon to make a bow. He has a roll of ribbon with $1\frac{7}{8}$ yards of ribbon. How much ribbon will be on the roll after Matteo makes a bow?

What operation should be used to find the amount of ribbon remaining?

_____

What is the difference between the numerators of the two

fractions? _____

What is the difference between the two fractions? _____

There is only one whole number in the problem. What is the next step to

solve? _____

Combine the whole number difference and fraction difference to find the

number of yards of ribbon remaining. _____

Write the fraction part of the answer in lowest terms.

What number are both the numerator and denominator divisible

by? _____

What is the fraction in lowest terms? _____

How much ribbon will be on the roll after Matteo makes the bow?

_____

> Add or subtract the numerators. The denominator stays the same.

> When a fraction is in lowest terms, the terms cannot be divided by a common number other than 1.

Use what you know about adding and subtracting fractions and mixed numbers to solve the problems below. Write the answers in lowest terms or as a mixed number.

1 $\frac{11}{12} - \frac{5}{12} =$ _____

3 $\frac{6}{8} + \frac{7}{8} =$ _____

2 $\frac{4}{9} + \frac{3}{9} =$ _____

4 $3\frac{3}{4} - 1\frac{1}{4} =$ _____

Solve the following problems.

1 Abby and Cheng are riding a Ferris wheel. The wheel turns $\frac{3}{10}$ of a full turn before stopping. After starting again, the Ferris wheel turns another $\frac{5}{10}$ of a full turn and stops again. What fraction of a full turn did the Ferris wheel turn in all? Write your answer in lowest terms. Show your work.

Remember to check if the numerator and denominator can be divided by the same number.

Answer _____ turn

2 A punch recipe calls for $4\frac{1}{3}$ cups of pineapple juice and $6\frac{2}{3}$ cups of orange juice. How much more orange juice than pineapple juice does the recipe call for? Show your work.

You can always check your answer by using the opposite operation.

Answer _____ cups

3 Jana is walking in an event to raise money for a hospital. She plans on walking $9\frac{7}{8}$ miles. She walks $4\frac{1}{8}$ miles before stopping for a snack. She walks another $2\frac{3}{8}$ miles before stopping again for water. How many miles does Jana have to walk before she is finished? Show your work.

Always make sure you have answered the question. Some problems involve more than one step.

Answer _____ miles

Solve the following problems.

1 Tyrese is making bran muffins. The recipe calls for $1\frac{1}{2}$ cups of wheat bran, $\frac{1}{2}$ cup of light brown sugar, 1 cup of flour, and $\frac{1}{2}$ cup of dark brown sugar to be mixed in a bowl. Tyrese will choose a bowl based on the total number of cups it can hold. What is the smallest number of cups the bowl he chooses must be able to hold?

Answer _____ cups

2 Which equations are correct? Select the **three** correct answers.

A $\frac{1}{6} + \frac{2}{6} = \frac{1}{2}$

B $6\frac{4}{5} - \frac{10}{5} = 5\frac{4}{5}$

C $4\frac{1}{5} + \frac{6}{5} = 4\frac{7}{10}$

D $3\frac{2}{3} - \frac{1}{3} = 3\frac{1}{3}$

E $\frac{12}{3} - \frac{8}{3} = 1\frac{1}{3}$

F $\frac{11}{4} + \frac{3}{4} = 1\frac{6}{8}$

3 A piece of paper is 11 inches long. Marisol folds the paper into 4 equal sections. She states that each section is $2\frac{2}{4}$ inches tall.

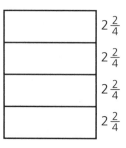

Part A Use addition or subtraction to determine if Marisol's measurements are correct. Explain how you know.

_____

_____

_____

Part B Marisol measures again and then correctly states that two of the sections of the paper are $\frac{11}{2}$ inches tall together. How much shorter was her total labeled measurements for the two sections than her new measurement for the two sections?

Answer _____ inch(es)

4 Ramona and Katie each ate $\frac{2}{5}$ of a box of cereal.

Part A How much of the box of cereal did they eat altogether? Draw a model to show your answer.

Answer _____ box

Part B Katie said that they ate $\frac{4}{10}$ of a box, while Ramona stated that they ate $\frac{8}{10}$ of a box. Are their fractions correct or incorrect? Explain how you know.

_____

_____

_____

_____

CCSS: 4.MD.1

Finding Equivalent Measurements

1 Introduction

There are two different systems of measurement, the **customary system** and the **metric system.** The customary system is used in the United States and a few other countries in the world. The metric system is used by most other countries.

The table shows some units of measurement in both systems. The units are arranged from smallest to largest in each measurement system.

MEASUREMENT UNITS

	Length	Capacity	Weight/Mass
Customary System	inch (in.) foot (ft) yard (yd) mile (mi)	cup (c) pint (pt) quart (qt) gallon (gal)	ounce (oz) pound (lb)
Metric System	centimeter (cm) meter (m) kilometer (km)	milliliter (mL) liter (L)	gram (g) kilogram (kg)

Use an appropriate unit for what you are measuring. Use small units to measure small things. For example, use inches or centimeters to measure the length of a finger.

Use medium units to measure medium things. For example, use quarts, gallons, or liters to measure the amount of water in a large water jug.

Use large units to measure large things. For example, use pounds or kilograms to measure how much a person weighs.

It is important to know and understand how measurement units relate when converting units.

MEASUREMENT EQUIVALENCE

	Length	Capacity	Weight/Mass
Customary System	1 ft = 12 in. 1 yd = 3 ft 1 yd = 36 in. 1 mi = 1,760 yd 1 mi = 5,280 ft	1 pt = 2 c 1 qt = 2 pt 1 gal = 4 qt 1 gal = 8 pt 1 gal = 16 c	1 lb = 16 oz
Metric System	1 m = 100 cm 1 km = 1,000 m	1 L = 1,000 mL	1 kg = 1,000 g

When converting from larger units to smaller units, multiply.

The height of a museum's ceiling is 9 yards. What is the height of the ceiling in feet?

Convert from a larger unit (yards) to a smaller unit (feet). There are 3 feet in each yard and the ceiling is 9 yards. Multiply.

$$3 \times 9 \text{ yd} = 27 \text{ ft}$$

Big → Small = Multiply
Small → Big = Divide

When converting from smaller units to larger units, divide.

A curtain panel is 180 centimeters long. How long is the panel in meters?

Convert from a smaller unit (centimeters) to a larger unit (meters). There are 100 centimeters in each meter. The panel is 180 centimeters long. Divide.

$$180 \text{ cm} \div 100 = 1.8 \text{ m}$$

Think About It

Look at the equivalence chart. Why do you think some of the measurements have more than one equivalent, such as miles? How is it possible to have more than one measurement they are equal to?

_____

_____

_____

2 Focused Instruction

Use the measurement units and equivalence charts to answer the questions.

➤ A giraffe is about 600 centimeters tall. Approximately, how tall is a giraffe in meters?

Is the question asking for smaller units or larger units? _____

Which operation should you use to find the height in meters?

_____

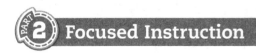

How many centimeters are in a meter? _____

Approximately, how tall is a giraffe in meters? _____

> Multiply to change to
> smaller units. Divide to
> change to larger units.

➤ A male giraffe has a mass of about 1,600 kilograms. What is the mass of a male giraffe in grams?

Is the question asking for smaller units or larger units?

_____

Which operation should you use to find the mass in grams?

_____

How many grams are in 1 kilogram? _____

Write an expression you can use to find the mass in grams.

_____

What is the approximate mass of a male giraffe, in grams?

_____

Work with a partner to measure the length of your classroom in yards, rounding to the nearest yard if needed. Then answer these questions.

What is the length of the classroom, in yards? _____

What operation can be used to convert the length from yards to feet?

_____

> Are yards larger or
> smaller than feet?

What operation can be used to convert from feet to inches?

_____

How many feet are in 1 yard? _____

How many inches are in 1 foot? _____

Write a multiplication expression that can be used to find the length of the

classroom, in inches. _____

What is the length of the classroom in inches? _____

Look at the measurement equivalence chart. What do you notice about the yard equivalence and the multiplication expression that you wrote?

_____

_____

Use what you know about measurements to answer these questions.

1 How many ounces are there in 6 pounds? _____

2 How many gallons are the same as 20 quarts? _____

3 A metal tub can hold 14 liters of water. How many milliliters of water can the

metal tub hold? _____

4 A jump rope is 300 centimeters long. How long is the jump rope in

meters? _____

Solve the following problems.

1 A punch bowl holds 2 gallons of punch. How many cups of punch does the punch bowl hold? Show your work.

> Gallons → Cups
> =
> Bigger → Smaller

Answer _____ cups

2 A butterfly flies 120 inches before landing on a flower. How far did the butterfly fly, in feet? Show your work.

> There are 12 inches in 1 foot.

Answer _____ feet

3 The distance from Kamal's school to his house is 6 kilometers. He calculated the distance in centimeters and found that the distance is 600 centimeters. Is he correct? Explain why or why not.

> Kilometers
> ↓
> Meters
> ↓
> Centimeters

_____

_____

_____

Solve the following problems.

1   Noah visited a bird sanctuary with his family. He recorded information he learned about some of the large birds of North America.

LARGE BIRDS OF NORTH AMERICA

Bird	Weight	Wingspan
Canada Goose	12 lb	60 in.
Great Horned Owl	3 lb	50 in.
California Condor	288 oz	3 yd
Turkey Vulture	5 lb	6 ft
American Bald Eagle	208 oz	90 in.

Part A   Which bird has the longest wingspan? Show your work.

Answer _____

Part B   If one of the birds is 16 ounces smaller than usual, which two birds would then have the same weight? Explain how you know.

_____

_____

_____

Part C   Noah wants to compare the birds' weights. He started this table to help him convert pounds to ounces. What mistake did Noah make?

Pounds	1	2	3	4	5
Ounces	16	32	44	64	80

_____

_____

2 Lira made a birdhouse. The birdhouse sits on a metal pole, 2 yards above the ground. How many inches above the ground is the birdhouse?

A 6

B 12

C 24

D 72

3 Taylor collected two rocks at the beach. One rock weighed 640 grams. The other rock weighed 330 grams more than the first rock. What is the combined weight, in kilograms, of both rocks? Show your work.

Answer _____ kilogram(s)

4 A small rain barrel can hold up to 40 gallons of water. Some potted plants need between 4 and 8 quarts of water per day, depending on how hot it is. If the rain barrel is full, what is the least and greatest number of days the plants can be watered without refilling the barrel? Explain your reasoning.

_____

_____

_____

_____

5 A clothing factory makes T-shirts. The table shows the amount of thread used for different numbers of shirts.

T-shirts	1	2	4	5	7
Thread (yards)	52	104	208	260	364

Circle an option in each set to make the following statement true.

According to the table, the factory needs [156,   624,   1,872,   5,616] inches of thread to make [2,   3,   5] T-shirts.

Big Ideas from Grade 4

CCSS: 4.NF.3, 6, 7; 4.NBT.5, 6; 4.MD.1

Solve the following problems.

1 The model below shows a multiplication problem.

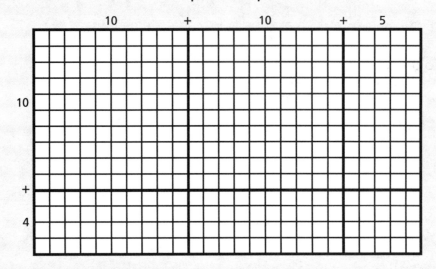

Write the multiplication problem and solve it using vertical multiplication.

Answer _____

2 Owen took some graham crackers to a camp-out. He ate $2\frac{1}{4}$ graham crackers on Friday. On Saturday, he had $1\frac{3}{4}$ graham crackers left to eat, but he dropped $\frac{1}{4}$ graham cracker. If he ate the remaining graham crackers, how many graham crackers did Owen eat altogether? Show your work.

Answer _____ graham crackers

3 Find the quotient of 3,656 ÷ 8.

Answer _____

4 What is the product of 502 × 3?

Answer _____

5 The table below shows the number of quarts in gallons.

Gallons	1	3	6		9
Quarts		12		28	36

Part A Complete the table by filling in the missing values.

Part B Using information in the table, how many quarts are equal to 25 gallons?

Answer _____ quarts

6 Which of the following fractions is the correct sum of $\frac{1}{8} + \frac{3}{8}$? Select the **two** correct answers.

A $\frac{4}{16}$

B $\frac{4}{8}$

C $\frac{2}{8}$

D $\frac{1}{2}$

E $\frac{2}{0}$

F $\frac{1}{4}$

7 A golf course charges $36 per round of golf. Eleven friends played golf. Out of the group, two friends forgot to bring money to play. If the remaining 9 friends split the cost of the 11 rounds of golf, how much more did they end up paying than if they had paid only for themselves? Show your work.

Answer $_____

8 Tovar read $\frac{2}{12}$ of a book last week. He also read the same amount over the weekend.

Part A Write an expression that could be used to find the part of the book Tovar had left to read.

Answer _____

Part B What fraction of the book did he have left to read?

Answer _____

9 Mark and label the approximate location of $\frac{96}{100}$ on the number line.

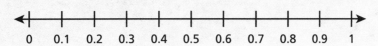

10 A large rectangular wall painting measures 96 inches long and
132 inches wide.

Part A What is the length and the width of the wall painting in feet?

Length _____ feet

Width _____ feet

Part B Explain how you found your answer.

_____

_____

11 Mark True or False for each of the following number sentences.

	True	False
0.40 > 0.4	☐	☐
$\frac{57}{100}$ < 0.6	☐	☐
0.1 < 0.13 < $\frac{14}{100}$	☐	☐

In grade 4, you compared decimals and multiplied and divided whole numbers. Now you can use what you know about decimals, multiplication, and division to work with place value and to add, subtract, multiply, divide, and compare decimals.

LESSON 5 Whole-Number Place Value In this lesson, you will determine place value, use base-ten blocks to model numbers, and explain the relationship between values.

LESSON 6 Powers of Ten In this lesson, you will use exponents, or powers, to represent the number of ones, tens, and hundreds in a number, and use the standard form to describe the number of zeros in the product.

LESSON 7 Decimal Names and Place Value In this lesson, you will write numbers in expanded form, add trailing and leading zeros where they apply, and use the products of place values.

LESSON 8 Comparing Decimals In this lesson, you will compare decimals by aligning the digits by place value and using place-value charts, and write comparison statements.

LESSON 9 Rounding Decimals In this lesson, you will round decimal numbers using the method you learned for rounding whole numbers. You will use what you know about place value to help you round decimals.

LESSON 10 Multiplying Whole Numbers In this lesson, you will multiply whole numbers using different methods.

LESSON 11 Dividing Whole Numbers In this lesson, you will divide whole numbers using different methods.

LESSON 12 Adding and Subtracting Decimals In this lesson, you will add and subtract decimals. You will regroup and use trailing and leading zeros to convert numbers.

LESSON 13 Multiplying Decimals In this lesson, you will multiply decimals. You will also use vertical multiplication and multiplication expressions to help you solve word problems.

LESSON 14 Dividing Decimals In this lesson, you will divide decimals by moving the decimal point, using vertical division, and adding a trailing zero after the decimal place.

Whole-Number Place Value

1 Introduction

The number system most commonly used is called a base-ten number system. The relationships between the digits in a base-ten number have a unique pattern as shown in the place-value chart.

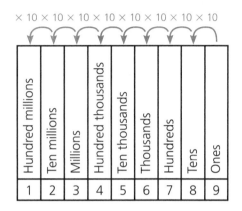

Each digit in a number has a **place value.** Place value determines how many ones, tens, hundreds, etc., there are in a number. Notice that as you move left, the place values increase by a factor of 10. As you move right along the place-value chart, each place value is $\frac{1}{10}$ of the value of the place to its left.

> Multiplying by $\frac{1}{10}$ is the same as dividing by 10.

In the number 233, there are 2 hundreds, 3 tens, and 3 ones.

The number 233 is the sum of all the values of each place, also called **standard form.** A number can also be written as an addition sentence that shows the digit in each place multiplied by the place value, called the **expanded form.** The value of each place in 233 is determined by its position in the number.

Expanded Form	Standard Form
$2 \times 100 + 3 \times 10 + 3 \times 1$	233

Think About It

Think about the numbers 387 and 3,087. Explain the relationship between the values of the digit 3 in both numbers as you go from the larger place value to the smaller one and from the smaller place value to the larger one.

_____

_____

_____

2 Focused Instruction

Use base-ten blocks to model the numbers and answer the questions.

➤ A family living in Boston takes two trips each year—a trip to Orlando, Florida, and a trip to Freeport, Maine.

  • Distance A: The distance from Boston to Orlando is about 1,286 miles.

  • Distance B: The distance from Boston to Freeport is about 128 miles.

The digit 2 is in which place in distance A? _____

Write the value of the 2 in distance A as a multiplication expression.

_____

The digit 2 is in which place in distance B? _____

Write the value of the 2 in distance B as a multiplication expression.

_____

How many times larger is the 2 in distance A than in distance

B? _____

Compare the values of the 1 in each of the distances.

Write a multiplication expression to determine the value of the 1 in

distance A. _____

Write a multiplication expression to determine the value of the 1 in distance B.

_____

> Write a multiplication expression to show the value of a digit using its place value.

What is the relationship between the value of the 1 in distance B to that of distance A? Explain how you know.

_____

_____

> A fraction can also represent division. For example, the fraction $\frac{1}{2}$ means to multiply by 1 then divide by 2.

To compare whole numbers, look at the digits in each place, starting on the left. Find the first place that the digits differ and compare the value of the digits.

➤ The United States Constitution was signed in the year 1787. The Declaration of Independence was signed in the year 1776.

Which two places have the same digit in both numbers?

_____

Which two places have different digits in both numbers?

_____

Which place in both numbers should be used to determine which

number is greater? _____

What is the value of the digit in that place in each number?

_____

> Start with the greatest place. Move towards the smaller places.

Which document was signed first? _____

Circle the second digit from the right in 1776. Circle the first digit on the right in 1787.

1776   1787

How many times greater is the circled digit in 1776 than the circled digit in 1787?

_____

The expanded form of a number shows the sum of the product of each digit in the number and the value of its place. Look at the expanded form of the two numbers shown below and answer the questions that follow.

$$(3 \times 1{,}000{,}000) + (8 \times 1{,}000) + (6 \times 100) + 9$$
$$(3 \times 1{,}000{,}000) + (8 \times 1{,}000) + (6 \times 10) + 9$$

What is the product of 3 and 1,000,000? _____

What is the product of 8 and 1,000? _____ 6 and

100? _____

What is the sum of the three products and 9?

_____

> Recall that the sum of the addends in expanded form is equal to the standard form.

Write the first number in standard form. _____

What is the product of 3 and 1,000,000? _____

What is the product of 8 and 1,000? _____ 6 and 10? _____

Write the second number in standard form. _____

What fraction of the value of the 6 in the first number is the 6 in the second

number? _____

How many times greater is the value of the 6 in the first number than in the

second number? _____

Use what you know about place value to write the numbers described below.

1   Write a number with three digits. Write a 4 in two places, making the 4 in one place have a value that is 10 times greater than the other 4.

_____

2   Write two four-digit numbers that use the digits 1, 3, 5, 7, or 8, in which the thousands digit of one number is 100 times greater than the tens digit of the other number.

_____

Solve the following problems.

1   At birth, a human baby has a total of 270 bones. This number decreases to 207 in some adults. How many times greater is the value of the 7 in 270 than in 207?

> How does the value of a place change as you move to the left?

Answer _____

2   There are about 8,337,000 people living in New York City. There are about 3,858,000 people living in Los Angeles. How many times greater is the place value of the 8 in the New York City population than the 8s in the Los Angeles population? Explain how you know.

> Think of the place value increasing by a certain factor in each place. There is a difference of 3 places in these numbers.

_____

_____

_____

3   The table below shows a list of items that K'Shawn's dad bought to build and furnish a deck.

Items Bought	Cost ($)
Table and Chairs	497
Chair Cushions	149
Deck Materials	1,975

Part A   What is the least expensive item K'Shawn's dad bought?

> Look at the place value of each digit.

Answer _____

Part B   What is the relationship between the 9 in the cost of the table and chairs and the 9 in the cost of the deck materials?

> Use the place value to determine the relationship.

_____

_____

Solve the following problems.

1 Alan is a DJ. He has 31,586 songs on his computer. He is asked to put together a list of 130 songs on a new playlist for students to select from at a school dance. What is the relationship between the values of the 3 in each number?

A   The value of the 3 in 31,586 is 10 times greater than in 130.

B   The value of the 3 in 31,586 is 100 times greater than in 130.

C   The value of the 3 in 31,586 is 1,000 times greater than in 130.

D   The value of the 3 in 31,586 is 10,000 times greater than in 130.

2 Mei-Ling wrote the numbers 2,314,508 and 2,358,104. She said that the value of 1 in the second number is 100 times greater than in the first number. Explain why Mei-Ling is incorrect and write the correct relationship using a fraction.

_____

_____

_____

_____

3 Mark True or False for each of the following statements.

	True	False
The value of 7 is 10 times greater in 704 than in 174.	☐	☐
The value of 2 is 1,000 times greater in 2,010 than in 1,020.	☐	☐
The value of 6 is $\frac{1}{10}$ the value in 15,678 than in 16,758.	☐	☐

4 Tarek buys a pomegranate with 314 seeds. He buys a second pomegranate that has more seeds. The number of seeds in the second pomegranate is made of the digits 6, 3, 1, and 4, but not in that order.

Part A If the value of 1 is 100 times greater in the second pomegranate, in what place should the 1 be written in the second number? Explain how you know.

_____

_____

_____

Part B The value of the 3 in the second number is $\frac{1}{10}$ the value of the 3 in the first number. The difference of the ones place and the tens place is equal to the difference of the hundreds place and the thousands. How many seeds does the second pomegranate have?

Answer _____ seeds

5 Which pair of numbers has 5 in places in which the value of one of the 5s is 10 times greater than in the other number?

  A   105 and 501

  B   6,450 and 3,952

  C   785 and 253

  D   534 and 195

LESSON 6 Powers of Ten

1 Introduction

In a base-ten number system, the digits 0–9 are used to represent the number of ones, tens, hundreds, and other places in a number. The number 10 does not appear as a digit by itself, so you regroup to make groups of tens, hundreds, thousands, and so on—all of which are groups of 10. Groups of 10 can also be seen as multiplying by 10s.

$$10 = 1 \text{ group of } 10 \rightarrow 10 = 10 \times 1$$
$$100 = 10 \text{ groups of } 10 \rightarrow 100 = 10 \times 10$$
$$1,000 = 100 \text{ groups of } 10 \rightarrow 1,000 = 10 \times 10 \times 10$$

Instead of writing many 10s multiplied by each other, you can use **exponents.** An exponent, or **power,** is a way of showing how many times to multiply a number by itself. The number being multiplied is called the **base.**

Base $\longrightarrow 5^2 \longleftarrow$ Exponent
$$5^2 = 5 \times 5$$

To write a repeated multiplication of 10, you can use the powers of 10, or 10 with an exponent, to describe how many times 10 is multiplied by itself.

$$10 = 10 \times 1 = 10^1$$
$$100 = 10 \times 10 = 10^2$$
$$1,000 = 10 \times 10 \times 10 = 10^3$$

Numbers with an exponent of 1 are equal to the base. Numbers with an exponent of 0 are equal to 1.
$$10^1 = 10$$
$$10^0 = 1$$

When multiplying a whole number by a power of 10, the product of the whole number and the power of 10 will be the same as the whole number with a certain number of zeros, described by the exponent, after it.

$$15 \times 10^1 = 150$$
$$15 \times 10^2 = 1,500$$
$$15 \times 10^3 = 15,000$$

When using powers of 10, you should note that the exponent also describes the number of zeros in the product, or **standard form,** of the number.

A similar pattern applies to multiplying decimals by a power of 10, in which the decimal point in the decimal number moves the number of spaces described by the exponent, to the right.

$$1.552 \times 10^1 = 15.52$$
$$1.552 \times 10^2 = 155.2$$
$$1.552 \times 10^3 = 1,552.$$

When dividing by powers of 10, the decimal point moves the number of spaces described by the exponent to the left.
$$1.552 \div 10^2 = 0.01552$$
$$1.552 \div 10^3 = 0.001552$$

Think About It

Predict the result of dividing a decimal number by a power of 10, such as $197.34 \div 10^3$. Prove your prediction using a calculator.

_____

_____

2 Focused Instruction

You can use expressions using powers of 10 to show very large or very small numbers.

➤ During a science project, Felix found that Earth is approximately $2{,}389 \times 10 \times 10$ miles from the moon. He wanted to write this distance using powers of 10 on a poster.

What is the number that will be multiplied by the power of 10? _____

How many 10s are in the expression? _____

What will the exponent need to be to describe the number of 10s being

multiplied? _____

What is the distance from Earth to the moon written as a multiplication

expression with powers of 10? _____

What is the value of 10×10? _____

The standard form is the product of the factors of the expression.

How many zeros will the standard form of the expression

have? _____

What is the standard form of the expression? _____

➤ To find the average number of times a person blinks in one year, a scientist uses the expression 6.25×10^6. The scientist finds the product of this expression as a number in standard form.

How many times is 6.25 multiplied by 10? _____

Rewrite the expression using factors of 10 instead of a power of 10.

_____

In what direction will the decimal point move? _____

How many places will the decimal point move? _____

What is the product of the expression? _____

➤ A grain of pollen has a diameter of about $9.75 \div 10^4$ inch.

How many times is 9.75 divided by 10? _____

What happens to the decimal point when dividing by powers of 10?

_____

How many places will the decimal point move? _____

What is the diameter of a grain of pollen? _____

> Does the decimal point move to the left or to the right?

Use what you know about powers of 10 to solve these problems.

1   Write the expression $10 \times 10 \times 10 \times 10 \times 10$ using an exponent. _____

2 $712 \times 10^3 =$ _____

3 $13.64 \times 10^7 =$ _____

4 $1,098.2 \div 10^4 =$ _____

Solve the following problems.

1 The speed of light can be written using the expression 3×10^8 meters per second. What is the speed of light written in standard form?

> What is the product of the expression?

Answer _____ meters per second

2 The average diameter of a grain of sand is 0.0024 inch.

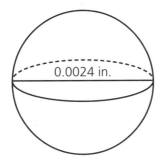

0.0024 in.

Part A What is the average diameter written as an expression with a whole number and a power of 10?

> What operation with a power of 10 will cause the decimal point to move left in a whole number?

Answer _____ inch

Part B Explain or show how the expression is correct.

_____

_____

_____

3 What happens to the decimal point when finding the product of 0.0038×10^4? What is the product?

> Will the decimal number increase or decrease when multiplied by the power of 10?

Answer _____

Solve the following problems.

1 There are about 100,000,000,000,000 cells in the human body. Which expressions can also be used to describe the average number of cells? Select the **two** correct answers.

A 1.0×10^5

B 1.0×10^{14}

C 1.0×10^{15}

D 0.1×10^6

E 0.1×10^{12}

F 0.1×10^{15}

2 What is the product of 0.065×10^2?

A 0.00065

B 0.0065

C 6.5

D 65

3 Look at the statements below.

- The distance from Earth to the sun is about 9.3×10^7 miles.
- The distance from Earth to Jupiter is about 3.65×10^8 miles.

What are the distances written in standard form? Explain how you know.

_____

_____

_____

_____

4 A red blood cell has a diameter of about $8.0 \div 10^3$ meter. Write directions that can be used by another student to find the standard form of the diameter of a red blood cell.

_____

_____

_____

5 Mark True or False for each of the following equations.

	True	False
$0.74 \times 10^5 = 7,400,000$	☐	☐
$12 \div 10^6 = 0.000012$	☐	☐
$497 \times 10^3 = 497,000$	☐	☐

6 Arun is a famous writer whose books earn a lot of money. He did not make much money on his first books, however.

Part A The first book Arun wrote earned him only 10^3 dollars. Write this number in standard form.

Answer _____

Part B Arun's most recent book earned 10^4 times as much money as his first book. How much did Arun's most recent book earn? Write the amount as a power of 10. Explain how you know your answer is correct.

_____

_____

_____

_____

7 A light-year is the distance that light can travel in a single year. There are 5.88×10^{12} miles in a light-year. The edge of the Milky Way Galaxy is about 2.5×10^6 light-years away from Earth.

Part A What is the distance that light can travel in a year, in standard form?

Answer _____ miles

Part B What is the distance from Earth to the edge of the Milky Way Galaxy, in light-years?

Answer _____ light-years

Decimal Names and Place Value

1 Introduction

Decimal numbers are based on the base-ten system. Each place has a value that is 10 times greater than the place to its right and $\frac{1}{10}$ the value of the place to its left. The table shows the number 2,222.222. Each 2 in this number has a different value because of its place in the number.

Thousands (× 1,000)	Hundreds (× 100)	Tens (× 10)	Ones	Decimal point	Tenths ($\times \frac{1}{10}$)	Hundredths ($\times \frac{1}{100}$)	Thousandths ($\times \frac{1}{1,000}$)
2	2	2	2	.	2	2	2

You can see the value of each 2 by writing the number in **expanded form.**

$$(2 \times 1,000) + (2 \times 100) + (2 \times 10) + (2 \times 1) + (2 \times \tfrac{1}{10}) + (2 \times \tfrac{1}{100}) + (2 \times \tfrac{1}{1,000})$$

↓	↓	↓	↓	↓	↓	↓
2,000	200	20	2	$\frac{2}{10}$	$\frac{2}{100}$	$\frac{2}{1,000}$

When naming a decimal number, you say the entire number after the decimal as if it were written as a whole number with the last place name at the end. So the number 2,222.222 is named as "two thousand, two hundred twenty-two and two hundred twenty-two thousandths."

> The word *and* is often replaced with the word *point* to represent the decimal point.

You can add a 0 to the end of a decimal number without changing its value. A 0 at the right end of a decimal number is called a **trailing zero.** For example, 0.4, 0.40, and 0.400 all have the same value. You can also add a **leading zero** without changing the value. This is a 0 in the ones place. So, .5 and 0.5 have the same value.

Zeros within a decimal number do affect the value of the number. For example, 1.98 and 1.908 are different numbers. These 0s are placeholders.

Think About It

A half-dollar coin has a diameter of 1.205 inches. Can the expanded form of the diameter be written with and without the 0? Explain how you know.

_____

_____

_____

2 Focused Instruction

Use a blank place-value chart to help answer each question.

➤ The tallest building in the world is the Burj Khalifa in Dubai, United Arab Emirates. It is 829.8 meters tall.

How many hundreds are in the number? _____

How many tens? _____ How many ones? _____

How many tenths? _____

What is the height written in expanded form?

_____

Use words to describe the name of the number.

_____

> Multiply the number in each place by the place value.

➤ Levon is sewing pants for a costume. The pins he uses to hold everything together are thirty-six thousandths inch in diameter.

Does the number have a fractional part and a whole number part? _____

Will the digits described be written to the left or right of the decimal point?

_____

What word describes the value of the rightmost place of the number?

_____

How many digits will be written to the right of the decimal point? _____

Write the diameter in standard form using a leading 0. _____

How many tenths are in the number? _____ How many hundredths?

_____ How many thousandths? _____

What is the diameter written in expanded form?

_____

Think about decimal place value and expanded form of numbers to answer each question.

➤ A gallon of water weighs $(8 \times 1) + (3 \times \frac{1}{10}) + (4 \times \frac{1}{100})$ pounds.

               ↓   ↓   ↓

           _____   _____   _____

> Multiply the whole number by the numerator to find the product and convert it to decimal form.

What is the product of each place in the expanded form, written in whole number or decimal form? Write the numbers in the spaces above.

How can you use the products of each place value to determine the standard

form of the weight? _____

What is the weight in standard form? _____

What is the weight of a gallon of water in words?

_____

Use what you know about decimal place value to write each number as described.

1 Expanded form: 132.907 _____

2 Standard form: $(6 \times 1{,}000) + (5 \times 10) + \left(8 \times \frac{1}{10}\right) + \left(4 \times \frac{1}{100}\right)$

   _____

3 Standard form: one hundred twenty-nine and three hundred eight

thousandths _____

Solve the following problems.

1 Shelby drove from Los Angeles to Seattle. The trip was
1,135.1 miles. What are the values of the 1s in this number?

> Write each place as the product of the digit and the place value.

_____

_____

_____

_____

_____

2 The diameter of a human hair is about one thousandth centimeter.
What is the diameter of a human hair written in expanded form?

> There is only one term in the expanded form.

Answer _____ centimeter

3 Will buys 5 cans of beans to make chili for a party. The cans contain
a total of $(2 \times 1) + (2 \times \frac{1}{100}) + (5 \times \frac{1}{1,000})$ kilograms of beans.
Will writes that there are 2.25 kilograms of beans for the chili. Is he
correct? Explain why or why not.

> Use zeros as placeholders where a place value is not shown in expanded form.

_____

_____

Solve the following problems.

1 A large grain of sand has a mass of 0.233 gram. Which forms also describe the grain of sand's mass? Select the **two** correct answers.

A two hundred thirty-three thousandths gram

B $(2 \times \frac{1}{10}) + (3 \times \frac{1}{10}) + (3 \times \frac{1}{100})$ gram

C two hundred thirty-three hundredths gram

D $(2 \times \frac{1}{10}) + (3 \times \frac{1}{100}) + (3 \times \frac{1}{1,000})$ gram

E two hundred and thirty-three hundredths gram

2 Amir writes the number 587.491 in expanded form but leaves out one of the digits by accident. The place value of the digit he leaves out is 100 times greater than the place value of the 9. Which digit did Amir forget to include, and how should the number be written in the expanded form? Explain how you know.

_____

_____

_____

3 Complete the expanded form of the number 810.703 below by filling in the boxes.

$$(8 \times 100) + \left(1 \times \boxed{}\right) + \left(\boxed{} \times \frac{1}{10}\right) + \left(3 \times \frac{\boxed{}}{\boxed{}}\right)$$

4 The radius of Earth's moon is about $(1 \times 1{,}000) + (7 \times 10) + (9 \times 1) + \left(6 \times \frac{1}{10}\right)$ miles. A moon for another planet has a different radius. That moon's radius is the same as Earth's moon except for the hundreds digit. The digit in the hundreds place for this planet's moon's radius is the same as the digit in the place that is $\frac{1}{10}$ the value of the hundreds place in Earth's moon's radius. What is the radius of the other moon in standard form?

Answer _____ miles

5 Look at the expanded form of a number shown.

$$(7 \times 1{,}000) + (3 \times 100) + (2 \times 10) + (6 \times 1) + \left(3 \times \frac{1}{10}\right) + \left(5 \times \frac{1}{1{,}000}\right)$$

Which digit is in a place with a value that is 100 times greater than the 5? Explain how you know.

_____

_____

6   The longest roller coaster in the world has a length of 2,478.938 meters.

   Part A   Label the place value of each digit in the number 2,478.938. Then
               write 2,478.938 in expanded form.

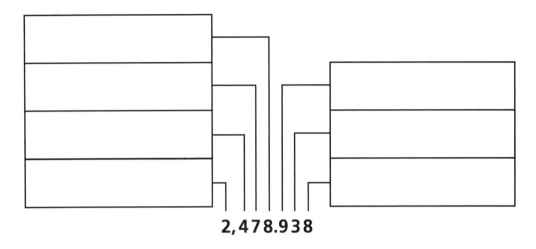

2,478.938

   Answer _____

   _____

   Part B   The digit 8 appears twice in the number 2,478.938. How do the
               values of the 8s compare?

   _____

   _____

   _____

   _____

Comparing Decimals

1 Introduction

Comparing numbers means deciding if one is greater than, equal to, or less than the other. Decimal numbers can be compared in much the same way as whole numbers.

In baseball, teams are assigned a win-loss percentage. These percentages are written as decimals. The win-loss percentage for baseball team A is 0.468 and for team B is 0.461. Which team has the greater percentage?

Compare the decimal numbers by aligning the digits by place value. Start by comparing the digits farthest to the left. If they are the same, compare the digits in the next place to the right. Continue until you reach digits that are different.

	Ones	Decimal Point	Tenths	Hundredths	Thousandths
Team A	0	.	4	6	8
Team B	0	.	4	6	1

- Ones are the same.
- Tenths are the same.
- Hundredths are the same.
- Thousandths are not the same.

Compare the first digits that are not the same, the thousandths. The digit in the thousandths place of the first number, 8, is greater than the thousandths digit of the second number, 1. So 0.468 is greater than 0.461. This means team A has the greater win-loss percentage.

Compare decimals with symbols instead of words. Comparison symbols include the **greater than (>), less than (<),** or **equal to (=)** symbols. A good way to remember the meaning of each symbol is to think of a hungry alligator. The alligator eats the bigger number.

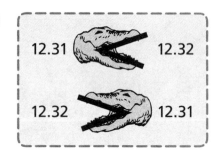

12.31 < 12.32

12.32 > 12.31

Compare the win-loss percentages above.

0.468 > 0.461

0.461 < 0.468

Think About It

Does a decimal number with more digits always have a greater value than a decimal number with fewer digits? Give an example to support your answer.

_____

_____

_____

 Focused Instruction

Look at each digit in the numbers you are comparing. Always start with the digits farthest to the left because they are the greatest.

➤ Nadia is comparing the cost of gasoline at two different gas stations.

STATION 1	STATION 2
Regular $3.31	Regular $3.29
Premium $3.42	Premium $3.43
Super $3.58	Super $3.59
per gallon	per gallon

She wonders which gas station is less expensive for each type of gas.

For regular gasoline, which place value should you look at to determine which station has the lower cost?

_____

> Look at the place values from left to right to find the first place in which the digits are different.

What are the digits in that place? _____

Which station has a lower cost for regular

gasoline? _____

For premium gasoline, which place value should you look at to determine which

station has the lower cost? _____

What are the digits in that place? _____

Which station has a lower cost for premium gasoline?

_____

For super gasoline, which place value should you look at to determine which

station has the lower cost? _____

What are the digits in that place? _____

Which station has a lower cost for super gasoline? _____

➤ A paper factory makes two thicknesses of paper. One paper is 0.002 inch thick
whereas the second type of paper is 0.003 inch thick.

Which place values have the same digit in both kinds of paper?

_____

Which place value has a different digit in both kinds of paper?

_____

Which digit is greater? _____

Which paper has the greater thickness? _____

Write the comparison using the > symbol. _____

How does the comparison change if you use the < symbol?

_____

> _ _ _ _ _ _ _ _ _ _
> | < means "is |
> | less than" |
> | > means "is |
> | greater than" |
> _ _ _ _ _ _ _ _ _ _

**Use what you know about decimal place values to answer these
questions.**

1 Complete the comparison by writing the appropriate symbol in the circle.

3.078 ◯ 3.18

2 Two runners completed a 10-kilometer race in 1.02 hours and 1.020 hours.
Write a comparison statement for these two running times.

_____

Solve the following problems.

1 During gym class, Gupta and Lee walked around the running track. Gupta walked 1.25 miles. Lee walked 1.52 miles. Which of the two boys walked a greater distance? Explain how you know.

> Compare the first digit that is different in each of the numbers.

_____

_____

_____

2 The table below shows the amount of fat per serving in five brands of pizza.

Brand	A	B	C	D	E
Fat Per Serving (in grams)	16.25	18.01	16.015	17.92	17.506

Amaya writes a comparison of the numbers as shown.

> Remember that the number of digits does not always determine the number with the greater value.

$$16.015 < 16.25 < 17.92 < 17.506 < 18.01$$

Is the comparison correct? Explain why or why not.

_____

_____

3 At the grocery store, Inez bought a loaf of bread for $2.65, a dozen eggs for $1.99, milk for $2.19, and a small bag of apples for $2.60. Order the prices from greatest to least.

> Stack the numbers to compare by place value.

Answer _____

Solve the following problems.

1   The times of four runners in a 100-meter sprint are shown in the table.

Runner	Time (sec)
Ty	12.328
Nam	12.02
Joe	12.325
Miguel	12.232

What is the order of runners as they finished the race?

Answer _____

2   Which set of numbers is in order from least to greatest? Select the **three** correct answers.

   A   15.018, 15.02, 15.023, 15.25, 15.030

   B   2.403, 2.411, 2.501, 2.505, 2.55

   C   31.009, 31.010, 31.11, 31.014, 31.104

   D   11.100, 11.135, 11.187, 11.988, 11.990

   E   8.207, 8.210, 8.215, 8.209, 8.218

   F   14.971, 14.977, 14.980, 14.991, 14.999

3 Marty visited the Insect Museum with his family. At the museum, he learned that beetles come in many sizes. Marty recorded some of the sizes of different beetle species he saw in a museum exhibit.

BEETLE LENGTHS

Beetle Species	Length (inches)
Flower beetle	0.167
Ladybug	0.092
Japanese beetle	0.6
Hercules beetle	6.75
Firefly	0.75

Part A Write the names of the beetles in order from shortest to longest.

Answer _____

_____

Part B A new beetle is added to the exhibit. It is shorter than a firefly, but longer than a Japanese beetle. Write a comparison that can be used to compare the length of the new beetle to the firefly and Japanese beetle. Use *b* to stand for the length of the beetle.

Answer _____

4 Mark True or False for each comparison.

	True	False
$107.32 > 107.302$	☐	☐
$68.15 < 68.150$	☐	☐
$204.800 = 204.8$	☐	☐

5 Ephraim is buying fruit at a market. The costs for fruit are shown.

Fruit	Cost (per pound)
Peaches	$1.91
Pears	$2.84
Plums	$1.94

Part A If Ephraim buys a pound of plums and a pound of peaches, which fruit will he spend more money on? Explain how you know.

_____

_____

Part B Write a comparison of the cost per pound of each type of fruit using a comparison symbol.

Answer _____

6 Circle an option in each set to make the following statement true.

The number 105.980 is [<, >, =] 105.99 because the digit in the

[ones, tenths, hundredths, thousandths] place in 105.980 is

[<, >, =] the digit in the same place in 105.99.

Rounding Decimals

Introduction

Rounding a whole number makes the number easier to work with when an exact answer is not needed. Decimal numbers are rounded using the same method and for the same reason as rounding whole numbers.

A piece of wooden trim is cut to decorate the outside of a new home. The trim measures 7.25 feet. What is the length of the trim rounded to the nearest whole number?

- Look at the place that you will be rounding to: the ones.   7.25

- Look at the digit to the right of that place.   7.25

- Round the digit in the ones place up if the underlined digit is 5 or greater. Keep the digit in the ones place the same if the underlined digit is 4 or less.

    $2 < 5$, so the colored digit will stay the same: 7.25 rounds to 7.

Use a number line to help you round decimals.

Notice on the number line that 7.25 is closer to 7 than it is to 8, so 7.25 rounds to 7.

Round the length of the trim to the nearest tenth.

$$7.2\underline{5} \rightarrow 7.3$$

Because the underlined digit is 5, the digit in the tenths place is rounded up to 3.

> Because the digit 5 is exactly between 0 and 10, a rule had to be written so that everyone rounded the same way.

Think About It

Write about a situation in which rounding might be helpful.

_____

_____

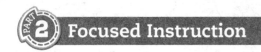

It is important to know the place values of the digits in numbers in order to round. Use circling and underlining or use a number line when rounding to help you answer these questions.

➤ Dasha paid $149.74 for water and electricity in August. She paid her bill to the nearest whole dollar. How much did Dasha pay the water and electricity company?

If the bill was paid in whole dollar amounts, what place did she round the bill to?

_____

Which place will determine if the value is rounded up or down?

_____

What is the digit in that place? _____

Will the place to be rounded round up or stay the same?

_____

How do you round 9 up?

_____

What is the whole dollar amount that Dasha paid? _____

> Rounding up a 9, requires regrouping, because 10 cannot be written in one place.

➤ It takes Viktor 14.35 minutes to walk from his house to the house of his friend Aaron. About how long does it take Viktor to walk to Aaron's house, to the nearest tenth of a minute?

14	14.05	14.1	14.15	14.2	14.25	14.3	14.35	14.4	14.45	14.5

Between which two tenths places is the number of minutes on the number line?

_____

Which tenths place does the number of minutes appear to be closer to?

_____

What does the digit in the hundredths place tell you to do with the digit in the

tenths place? _____

What is the number of minutes rounded to the nearest tenth? _____

You can use rounded numbers to solve problems. Round first. Then add, subtract, multiply, or divide.

➤ On her first birthday, Tina was 0.791 yard tall. On her 15th birthday, Tina was 1.837 yards tall. To the nearest hundredth, how much did Tina grow between these birthdays?

To what place does the problem ask you to round?

_____

What place is to the right of the tenths?

Which digit in Tina's height at age 1 will tell you how to round? _____

What was Tina's height at age 1, rounded to the nearest hundredth?

_____

Which digit in Tina's height at age 15 will tell you how to round? _____

What was Tina's height at 15, rounded to the nearest hundredth?

_____

What operation should you use to find by how much Tina's height changed?

_____

Write and solve a number sentence to find how much Tina grew.

_____

Use what you know about rounding decimals to solve these problems.

1 Round each number to the nearest hundredth.

   a 47.901 _____   **b** 19.768 _____   **c** 3.254 _____

2 Round each number to the nearest tenth.

   a 95.104 _____   **b** 5.679 _____   **c** 4.468 _____

3 Round each number to the nearest whole number.

   a 378.21 _____   **b** 19.73 _____   **c** 125.56 _____

Solve the following problems.

1 Ali is buying a new computer. He compares the prices of two computers. One laptop will cost him $873.96, while a different laptop will cost him $884.15. To the nearest dollar, how much more will the more expensive laptop cost than the other? Show your work.

> Round before finding the difference.

Answer $_____

2 Ellis walks to school. He lives 0.845 mile from school. To the nearest tenth, how far does Ellis walk to school?

> What place should you look at to round to the nearest tenth?

Answer _____ mile

3 At the veterinarian, Shay's dog is put on a scale. The dog weighs 14.67 pounds. The veterinarian writes 15 pounds on the dog's medical report. Explain how the veterinarian rounded the weight.

> Think about how a decimal number is rounded to the nearest whole number.

_____

_____

_____

Solve the following problems.

1 Latisha and Cameron competed in a 100-meter butterfly swim race. Latisha finished in 53.82 seconds. Cameron finished in 51.65 seconds. To the nearest tenth of a second, what were the finishing times for each girl?

Latisha _____ seconds

Cameron _____ seconds

2 Which number is the result of rounding 209.808 to the nearest whole number?

A 209

B 209.80

C 209.91

D 210

3 Which decimal rounds up when rounded to the hundredths place? Select the **three** correct answers.

A 89.327

B 89.237

C 89.372

D 89.322

E 89.732

F 89.727

4 Colin is preparing a pamphlet for a city housing agency. The pamphlet tells residents about the choices for electric service. Colin's pamphlet lists the five companies that supply electricity in his city. To make the rates easier to compare, Colin wants to round each rate to the nearest hundredth.

Part A Complete the table by rounding each decimal to the hundredths place.

Electricity Company	Rate Charged (cents per kilowatt-hour)	Rate Rounded to the Nearest Hundredth
Atlas Energy	12.065	
Big City Light	9.138	
Connex	9.143	
Dynamon Power	9.707	
ElectriCo	9.503	

Part B According to the rounded rates, which company (or companies) has the lowest rate?

Answer _____

Part C Explain how two companies that charge different rates can have the same rate when their rates are rounded to the hundredths.

_____

_____

_____

_____

5 When rounding 72.631 to the hundredths place, Jack rounded to 72.64 and Tamar rounded to 72.63. Who is correct? Explain your answer.

_____

_____

6 Look at the statement below.

$$149.95 \rightarrow 150.0$$

Explain how 149.95 becomes 150 when rounding to the nearest tenth.

_____

_____

_____

1 Introduction

Multiplication combines groups of equal size. An **array** is an organized way of showing multiplication.

A concert ticket costs $15. If you buy 5 tickets, how much will you spend?

The array shows a dot for each dollar. There are 5 rows because there are 5 tickets. There are 15 dots in each row because each ticket costs $15.

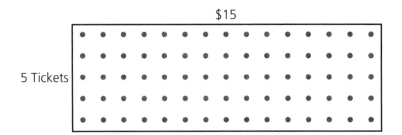

$15

5 Tickets

> The answer you get when you multiply is known as the **product.** The numbers being multiplied are the **factors.**

There are 75 dots in the array because 5 × 15 = 75.

For larger numbers, it is faster to stack the factors and multiply vertically.

Multiply the ones value of 15 and both digits of 50, or 5 × 50.

$$\begin{array}{r} 50 \\ \times 15 \\ \hline 250 \end{array}$$ ← Partial Product

Multiply the tens value of 15 and both digits of 50, or 10 × 50.

$$\begin{array}{r} 50 \\ \times 15 \\ \hline 250 \\ 500 \end{array}$$ ← Partial Product
← Partial Product

Add the partial products to find the product.

$$\begin{array}{r} 50 \\ \times 15 \\ \hline 250 \\ 500 \\ \hline 750 \end{array}$$ ← Product

Think About It

If a three-digit number were multiplied by a three-digit number, how many partial products would need to be added? Explain how you know.

_____

_____

_____

2 Focused Instruction

Work with a partner. Use grid paper to model and solve the problem.

➤ A cake decorator is making colored sugar squares to cover the top of a cake. There are 12 rows with 14 squares in each row.

Draw a grid that shows the top of the cake. Use the space below or your grid paper.

How can you find the number of squares in the grid?

_____

Write a multiplication expression that can be used to find the number of squares.

_____

How many squares will be used on top of the cake? _____

Which method is faster, counting the squares or multiplying?

_____

Use vertical multiplication to solve the problem below and answer the questions that follow.

➤ There are 185 classrooms at a large school. Each of the classrooms can hold 23 students. How many students can the classrooms hold in all?

In the space at right, write the multiplication problem vertically.

How many partial products will there be? _____

What is the first partial product? _____

What is the second partial product? _____

What is the sum of the partial products? _____

Use what you know about multiplying numbers to solve these problems.

1 $13 \times 38 =$ _____

2 $102 \times 29 =$ _____

3 $586 \times 211 =$ _____

4 $27 \times 1,214 =$ _____

Solve the following problems.

1 Find the product. Show your work.

$$94 \times 60 = \square$$

> Align the factors vertically by place value.

Answer _____

2 Kayin is collecting canned food for donations to a shelter. He has 22 boxes that can each hold 24 cans. If he collects enough food to completely fill the boxes, how many cans will he collect? Show your work.

> How many partial products will you find?

Answer _____ cans

3 Look at the multiplication problem and solution below.

```
   381
  ×101
   381
   000
  3810
  4191
```

> Think about how many digits each partial product should have.

The calculation is incorrect. In which steps were the errors made? Explain how you know.

_____

_____

_____

_____

Solve the following problems.

1   An adult human heart beats an average of 72 times per minute. With each
    beat, it pumps 70 milliliters of blood. How many milliliters of blood does the
    average human heart pump in 1 minute? Show your work.

Answer _____ milliliters

2   Ling Li has 16 bags of mini crackers. Each bag has 24 crackers.

   Part A   What is the total number of mini crackers Ling Li has?

   Answer _____ crackers

   Part B   Explain how you know your answer is correct. Tell how you found
              your answer and why you chose this method.

   _____

   _____

   _____

3   Write the letter of the correct product after each expression.

   357×116 _____

   81×75 _____

   109×54 _____

   518×26 _____

   69×33 _____

   $21 \times 2,038$ _____

a. 6,075
b. 13,468
c. 42,798
d. 2,277
e. 41,412
f. 5,886

4 A giant panda may eat as much as 14 kilograms of bamboo in a single day.

Part A How many kilograms of bamboo will a giant panda eat in a year of 365 days? Explain how you found the answer.

_____

_____

_____

Part B Tokyo's Ueno Zoo received a pair of giant pandas from China in 2011. How many kilograms of bamboo does the zoo need to have to be prepared to feed the pandas for any single month? Explain how you found your answer.

_____

_____

_____

_____

5 Darius practices playing the drums for 55 minutes, 2 days a week. He practices every week without missing any practice sessions. To determine the number of minutes he practices each year, he writes the expression shown below.

$$(50 \times 4) + (50 \times 100) + (5 \times 4) + (5 \times 100)$$

Will the expression correctly determine the number of minutes he will practice each year? Why or why not?

_____

_____

_____

6   The multiplication problem below is missing digits.

$$
\begin{array}{r}
7\ \ 2\ \ 0 \\
\times \underline{}\ \ 9 \\
\hline
\underline{}\ \ 4\ \ 8\ \ 0 \\
2\ \ 8\ \ 8\ \ 0\ \ 0 \\
\hline
\underline{}\ \underline{}\ \underline{}\ \ 8\ \ 0
\end{array}
$$

Part A   Complete the multiplication problem by filling in the missing digits.

Part B   Explain how you found the missing digits in Part A.

_____

_____

_____

_____

_____

LESSON 11 Dividing Whole Numbers

1 Introduction

Division is used to separate a set of objects into groups that are equal. You can use long division to solve problems.

> A shipment of 450 pounds of cat litter was sent to a pet supply store. The litter was in bags that hold 15 pounds each. How many bags of cat litter did the store receive?

Set up a division problem using a division box: 15)450

Divide 45 by 15 because 4 is not divisible by 15. Write a 3 above the 5 in 45.

$$\begin{array}{r} 30 \\ 15\overline{)450} \\ \underline{45} \\ 00 \\ \underline{0} \\ 0 \end{array}$$

Multiply 15 by 3 and write 45 below the dividend. Subtract 45 from 45.

Bring down the 0.

Divide 0 by 15 and write 0 above the 0 in 450.

Multiply 0 by 15 and write a 0 below 00. Subtract 0 from 0.

Since there is nothing left to bring down, the problem is finished. The quotient is 30.

The store received 30 bags with 15 pounds of cat litter in each.

> The **dividend** is the number being divided. The **divisor** is the number doing the dividing. The **quotient** is the answer.

> For every long division problem, remember:
> 1. Divide
> 2. Multiply
> 3. Subtract
> 4. Bring down

Think About It

If the divisor is a two-digit number, can you write a rule for how many digits in the dividend you will need to look at to complete the first step in dividing? Explain your answer.

_____

_____

_____

_____

UNIT 2 Number and Operations in Base Ten **85**

© The Continental Press, Inc.   DUPLICATING THIS MATERIAL IS ILLEGAL.

Multiplication is the opposite of division. You can use multiplication to check your answer to division problems.

➤ Nathan orders a pallet of stone for a backyard project. A pallet of stone weighs 1,080 pounds. Nathan's wheelbarrow can carry 60 pounds of stone at one time. Nathan must move the stone from the front yard to the backyard using his wheelbarrow.

Use long division to solve the problem.   60)‾1,080

> What is the first place into which 60 can divide?

Does 60 divide into 1? _____

Does 60 divide into 10? _____

Does 60 divide into 108? _____

How many times does 60 go into 108? _____

How many are left? _____

How many times does 60 divide into this number? _____

How many are left? _____

How many trips will Nathan have to make with the wheelbarrow? _____

How can you use multiplication to check your answer?

_____

_____

➤ Hattie has $286 with which to buy turkeys for the Thanksgiving community supper. The turkeys are on sale for $22 each.

Write a division expression that can be used to find how many turkeys Hattie

could buy if she spends all the money she has. _____

Does 22 divide into 2? _____

Does 22 divide into 28? _____

How many times? _____

What number should be subtracted from 28? _____

What is the remaining number that needs to be divided? _____

How many times does 22 go into that number? _____

What is the quotient? _____

How many turkeys can Hattie buy? _____

Prove your answer is correct showing the long division.

Use what you know about long division to solve these problems.

1 209 ÷ 11 = _____

2 544 ÷ 32 = _____

3 5,265 ÷ 81 = _____

4 657 ÷ 9 = _____

Solve the following problems.

1 An aquarium has a sea horse tank that holds 2,025 liters. There are 25 liters of water per sea horse to give them enough space. How many sea horses can fit in the tank if it is completely full? Show your work.

> You will need to divide the first three digits of the dividend.

Answer _____ sea horses

2 A bike repair shop orders a shipment of new tire inner tubes. Each inner tube costs $16. If the shipment costs $544, how many inner tubes did the shop order? Show your work.

> Divide → Multiply → Subtract → Bring Down

Answer _____ inner tubes

3 Adult female gorillas eat 15 kilograms of plants each day. An animal protection facility is caring for a female gorilla before she is sent back into the wild. The gorilla eats 855 kilograms during her stay at the facility and 90 kilograms while she is traveling back to the wild. How many days passed before the gorilla was back in the wild? Explain how you know.

> You will need to find the total amount eaten first.

_____

_____

Solve the following problems.

1 Riders in the 2010 Tour de France bicycled about 3,580 kilometers. The race began on July 4 and ended on July 25. Riders had 2 days off during the tour.

Part A   Which statements correctly describe how many kilometers the riders biked on each day they raced? Select the **two** correct answers.

  A   The race was 22 days long. The distance per day was
  3,580 ÷ (22 − 2) days = 179 kilometers.

  B   The riders biked for 21 days. The distance per day was
  3,580 ÷ 21 days = 170 kilometers.

  C   The race was 21 days long. The distance per day was
  3,580 ÷ (21 − 2) days = 188 kilometers.

  D   The riders biked for 20 days. The distance per day was
  3,580 ÷ 20 days = 179 kilometers.

  E   The riders biked for 19 days. The distance per day was
  3,580 ÷ 19 days = 188 kilometers per day.

  F   The race was 23 days long. The distance per day was
  3,580 ÷ (23 − 2) days = 170 kilometers.

Part B   A rider rode 5 kilometers more than the average number of kilometers per day during one day of the race. If he had an average speed of 23 kilometers per hour on that day, how many hours did he ride? Explain how you know.

_____

_____

_____

2 The greatest amount of rainfall recorded to date was in January 1966 on an island in the Indian Ocean. The island had about 72 inches of rainfall in a 24-hour period. How many inches per hour fell during that period? Check your work using multiplication.

Answer _____ inches per hour

3 As of 2014, the country of Austria had won 18 gold medals and 33 silver medals during the Summer Olympics. The silver medals have a total mass of 17,325 grams. Both the silver and gold medals have a total mass of 26,883 grams. What is the mass of each gold medal? Explain how you know.

_____

_____

_____

4 Complete the division problem by filling in the missing digits.

```
            __  4  7
    1  9) 2  7  9  3
           1  9
              8 __
          _____
              1  3  3
              1  3  3
                    0
```

5 A river is threatening to flood a small town. Volunteers are filling sandbags and piling them along a riverbank. Each full sandbag weighs about 37 pounds. A truck unloads 3,150 pounds of sand. About how many sandbags can be filled from this load of sand?

Answer _____ sandbags

6 In order to lose 1 pound, a person needs to burn about 3,600 more calories than he or she eats and drinks. A person who weighs 155 pounds burns about 240 calories per hour by walking at a moderate pace.

Part A About how many minutes would a 155-pound person have to walk at a moderate pace in order to lose 1 pound?

Answer _____ minutes

Part B Explain how you found your answer.

_____

_____

_____

_____

Part C Lionel weighs 155 pounds. He starts a walking program. How many minutes a day would Lionel have to walk at a moderate pace in order to lose 1 pound in 30 days? Show your work.

Answer _____ minutes

LESSON 12 Adding and Subtracting Decimals

1 Introduction

Adding and subtracting decimals is done using the same method as adding and subtracting whole numbers. When adding and subtracting decimals, you align the place values and the decimal points.

Aidan spent $73.85 on a new skateboard. He also bought a new helmet for $42.97. How much did Aidan spend on his new skateboard and helmet?

Add the hundredths.	Add the tenths.	Add the ones.	Add the tens.
$\begin{array}{r} 1 \\ 73.85 \\ +\ 42.97 \\ \hline 2 \end{array}$	$\begin{array}{r} 1\ 1 \\ 73.85 \\ +\ 42.97 \\ \hline 82 \end{array}$	$\begin{array}{r} 1\ 1 \\ 73.85 \\ +\ 42.97 \\ \hline 6.82 \end{array}$	$\begin{array}{r} 1\ 1 \\ 73.85 \\ +\ 42.97 \\ \hline 116.82 \end{array}$

Aidan spent a total of $116.82 on his new skateboard and helmet.

Solve decimal subtraction problems in the same way the above addition problem was solved.

Aidan gave the cashier at the skate shop $120.85 in cash. How much change did the cashier give Aidan?

Subtract the hundredths.	Subtract the tenths.	Subtract the ones.	Subtract the tens.	Subtract the hundreds.
$\begin{array}{r} 120.85 \\ -116.82 \\ \hline 3 \end{array}$	$\begin{array}{r} 120.85 \\ -116.82 \\ \hline .03 \end{array}$	$\begin{array}{r} {}^{1\,10} \\ 1\cancel{2}0.85 \\ -116.82 \\ \hline 4.03 \end{array}$	$\begin{array}{r} {}^{1\,10} \\ 1\cancel{2}0.85 \\ -116.82 \\ \hline 04.03 \end{array}$	$\begin{array}{r} {}^{1\,10} \\ 1\cancel{2}0.85 \\ -116.82 \\ \hline 004.03 \end{array}$

The differences of the tens and hundreds places are equal to 0. The leading zeros do not have a value, so Aidan received $4.03 back from the cashier.

> Regroup if a place value is not large enough to find the difference.

Think About It

Explain how you would subtract a decimal from a whole number.

_____

_____

_____

_____

2 Focused Instruction

Be sure to line up decimals correctly when adding and subtracting. Always add or subtract digits in the same place.

➤ Tran has a turtle with a mass of 0.75 kilogram and a turtle with a mass of 0.4 kilogram. What is the total mass of the two turtles?

What is the number name of 0.75? _____

What is the number name of 0.4? _____

What digit is in the hundredths place in 0.4? _____

Which digits will you add to add the hundredths?

_____

Use vertical addition to find the sum of 0.75 and 0.4.

What is the sum of 0.75 and 0.4? _____

_____

➤ During gym class, Keesha ran a mile in 10.2 minutes. Reki ran a mile in 0.84 minute less than Keesha. How fast did Reki run a mile?

What is the problem asking you to find?

_____

> Add a trailing zero to 0.4 to convert it to hundredths.

How can you subtract decimals that do not have the same number of decimal places?

_____

Write the subtraction problem using vertical subtraction.

Can you subtract 4 from 0? _____

Explain what you must do first in order to subtract 4.

_____

_____

What is the difference in the hundredths place?

_____

Can you subtract 8 tenths from 1 tenth? _____

What must you do before you are able to subtract?

_____

_____

What is the difference in the tenths place? _____

What is the difference in the ones place? _____

How long did it take Reki to run a mile? _____

Use what you know about adding and subtracting decimals to solve these problems.

1 134.57 + 19.71 = _____

2 46.09 − 28.1 = _____

Solve the following problems.

1   Tuesday's low temperature of 50.7°F came just before dawn. During the day, the temperature increased 23.9°F. What was Tuesday's high temperature? Show your work.

Increased refers to the temperature rising.

Answer _____°F

2   The average house sparrow weighs 1.39 ounces. The house sparrow weighs 0.53 ounce more than the Eurasian tree sparrow. What is the weight of a Eurasian tree sparrow? Show your work.

The words *more than* suggest you need to find a difference.

Answer _____ ounce(s)

3   Every month Marina pays $79 for mobile phone service, $59.95 for cable service, and $45.50 for Internet service. She can switch to a plan that charges $129.99 a month for all three services. On that plan, how much money would Marina save monthly? Explain how you found your answer.

How much is Marina paying for all of her monthly services?

_____

_____

_____

Solve the following problems.

1   A plumber is fixing a pipe with an interior diameter of 0.63 inch. He buys a replacement piece that must fit inside the old pipe. He uses plumbing tape that will fill 0.15 inch of the space between the two pieces of pipe. The new pipe must be 0.1 inch smaller than the old pipe and tape, so that it can fit inside.

Part A   What is the largest interior diameter pipe he can buy that will still fit inside the old pipe?

Answer _____ inch

Part B   Explain how you found your answer.

_____

_____

_____

2   Which expressions are equivalent to 2.37? Select the **three** correct answers.

A   4.44 − 2.07

B   1.99 + 0.48

C   17.14 − 14.87

D   33.1 − 30.73

E   0.98 + 1.49

F   0.56 + 1.81

3 The table below shows the 2010 population data for the three largest countries in North America.

Country	2010 Population
Canada	33.89 million
Mexico	110.65 million
United States	317.64 million

Part A How many more people lived in the United States than in Mexico and Canada combined? Explain how you know.

_____

_____

_____

Part B The total population of the two most populated states in the United States was 30.81 million greater than the entire population of Canada. If the state with the largest population in the United States had 38.3 million people, what was the population of the second greatest populated state? Explain how you know.

_____

_____

_____

_____

4 The areas of three rooms in Mr. Cheng's house are shown below.

- Bathroom = 64.75 square feet

- Kitchen = 102.29 square feet

- Bedroom = 317.89 square feet

Complete the statement below.

The area of Mr. Cheng's bedroom is _____ square feet greater than the total square footage of his kitchen and bathroom.

5 The Men's 4 × 100-Meters Medley Relay is an Olympic event in which each
   member of a 4-person team swims 100 meters. In the 2012 Summer
   Olympics, a US team won the gold medal with a combined time of 3 minutes
   29.35 seconds. The first three swimmers' times were 52.58 seconds,
   59.19 seconds, and 50.73 seconds. What was the fourth swimmer's time?
   Explain how you found your answer.

   _____

   _____

   _____

LESSON
13 Multiplying Decimals

1 Introduction

When multiplying decimals, you are finding a part of a part.

To model multiplying decimals, you can shade two areas of the same grid.

Find the product of 0.6×0.5.

The green on the grid shows 0.6. The gray shows 0.5. Notice that the green and gray overlap. This part represents the product of 0.6×0.5. There are 30 squares shaded with both colors, which is $\frac{30}{100}$ of the grid.

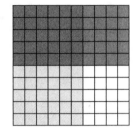

$$0.6 \times 0.5 = 0.3 \qquad \frac{30}{100} = 0.3$$

Decimals can also be multiplied in the same way that whole numbers are multiplied. The product has the same number of decimal places as the sum of the decimal places in the factors.

> Find area of a rectangle by multiplying length and width.

A rectangular deck measures 8.25 feet long and 27.5 feet wide. What is the area of the deck?

Multiply 5 × 275.	Multiply 20 × 275.	Multiply 800 × 275.	Add the partial products.
3 2 27.5 ×8.25 —— 1375	1 1 27.5 ×8.25 —— 1375 5500	64 27.5 ×8.25 —— 1375 5500 220000 ——	1375 5500 +220000 ———— 226875

The number 27.5 has one decimal place and 8.25 has two decimal places, so the product will have three decimal places. The deck is 226.875 square feet.

Think About It

If a product has four decimal places and both factors have the same number of decimal places, how many decimal places does each of the factors have? Explain your reasoning.

_____

_____

_____

② Focused Instruction

Using grids helps you see the multiplication. Be careful that you shade the correct number of squares. One factor should be shaded horizontally and the other should be shaded vertically. Look at the grid below and answer the questions that follow.

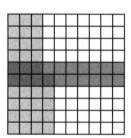

> Recall that each square in the grid represents 0.01 or $\frac{1}{100}$.

How many squares are green, including squares that are both green and gray?

_____

What decimal number is modeled by the green squares? _____

How many squares are gray, including squares that are both green and gray?

_____

What decimal number is modeled by the gray squares? _____

Write a multiplication expression that is modeled by the grid.

_____

How many squares are both green and gray? _____

What decimal number is modeled by the green and gray squares? _____

What is the product modeled by the grid? _____

Find the product of the two factors using vertical multiplication.

Is the product of the vertical multiplication the same as the modeled problem?

_____

Think of multiplying decimals as multiplying whole numbers. Place the decimal point after you find the product.

➤ Earth is 149.6 million kilometers from the sun. Mars is about 1.52 times farther from the sun.

Write a multiplication expression that can be used to find the distance from Mars

to the sun. _____

Write the first step in the multiplication of the two decimals as a multiplication expression using two whole numbers.

_____

What is the product of the two factors? _____

Write the second step in the multiplication of the two decimals as a

multiplication expression using two whole numbers. _____

What is the product of the two factors? _____

Write the third step in the multiplication of the two decimals as a multiplication

expression using two whole numbers. _____

What is the product of the two factors? _____

Multiply using vertical multiplication.

> What numbers do you multiply first?

What do you notice about the partial products in the vertical multiplication and in the steps on the previous page?

_____

What is the sum of the partial products? _____

What is the distance from Mars to the sun?

_____

Use what you know about decimal multiplication to find these products.

1 $5.67 \times 1.98 =$ _____

2 $3.1 \times 46.06 =$ _____

3 $0.36 \times 9.2 =$ _____

4 $2.751 \times 8.56 =$ _____

Solve the following problems.

1 The final bill at a restaurant is $38.59. The restaurant charges a tax equal to
   0.08 of the bill. What is the total tax on the bill? Give your answer to the
   nearest hundredth. Show your work.

> The word *of*
> generally refers to
> multiplication in
> word problems.

Answer $_____

2 A pay-per-use cellphone charges $0.20 per text message sent or received. If
   Dorian sent and received a total of 124 texts in one month, how much will
   Dorian pay for the text messages? Show your work.

> Align the
> numbers just as if
> they were both
> whole numbers.

Answer $_____

3 An artist uses pieces of ribbon that measure 2.4 inches in length for a project.
   The project uses 50 lengths of ribbon. What total length of ribbon will be
   used for the project? Show your work.

> Does the order of the
> factors in the vertical
> multiplication change
> the product?

Answer _____ inches

Solve the following problems.

1   Dana installed a new toilet that uses 1.6 gallons of water per flush. Her old
toilet used 3.1 times as much water. How much water did Dana's old toilet
use per flush? Show your work.

Answer _____ gallons

2   Brona works on a 6.4-acre farm. Corn is grown on 0.32 of the farm's area.
Tomatoes are grown on 0.25 of the farm's area.

Part A   What area, in acres, of the farm is used for corn and tomatoes?

Answer _____ acres

Part B   Explain how you found your answer.

_____

_____

_____

_____

3   Lake Baikal in Russia holds 23.6 trillion cubic meters of water. The amount of
freshwater on Earth is about 5.02 times greater than the amount of water in
Lake Baikal.

Complete the statement below.

There are about _____ trillion cubic meters of freshwater on Earth.

4 The average person in the United States consumes 0.2 kilogram of tea per year. The average person in China consumes 2 times that amount. The average person in Turkey consumes 4 times as much tea as the average person in China.

Part A How much tea does the average person in Turkey consume per year? Show your work.

Answer _____ kilograms

Part B To find the answer, Tomás multiplies 2 × 4 = 8 and then multiplies 0.2 by 8. Will he get the same answer? Explain.

_____

_____

_____

5 Teji solved the problem shown below.

$$
\begin{array}{r}
11.95 \\
\times 8.06 \\
\hline
7170 \\
000000 \\
+\ 95600 \\
\hline
1027.70
\end{array}
$$

Part A He made two mistakes: one format error and one calculation error. What errors did Teji make in his solution?

_____

_____

Part B Describe how to fix the errors and give the correct product.

_____

_____

_____

6 Mark True or False for each of the following equations.

	True	False
$0.3 \times 0.04 = 0.12$	☐	☐
$1.5 \times 0.2 = 0.3$	☐	☐
$0.07 \times 6 = 0.42$	☐	☐
$5.0 \times 8.1 = 4.05$	☐	☐

7 Bai-Ling is staining a concrete patio that measures 9.38 feet by 10.625 feet.

Part A What is the area of the patio if each measurement is rounded to the nearest tenth? Show your work.

Answer _____ square feet

Part B A can of stain covers 20 square feet and costs $32.95 per can. To the nearest whole number, about how much will Bai-Ling spend on stain for her patio? Explain how you know.

_____

_____

_____

_____

LESSON
14 Dividing Decimals

1 Introduction

To divide decimals, use a very similar method to the one you use for dividing whole numbers.

Olina is raising money by selling lemonade. She made $5.75 on her first day. If she makes $0.25 from each cup she sells, how many cups of lemonade did she sell on her first day?

To find the number of cups of lemonade Olina sold, divide the total amount of money she earned by the amount she earned for each cup.

First, write the problem using a division symbol: $0.25\overline{)5.75}$.

Move the decimal point in the divisor to the right to divide by a whole number rather than a decimal. There are two decimal places in the divisor, so the decimal point also moves two places in the dividend.

$$0.25\overline{)5.75} \rightarrow 25\overline{)575}$$

> Moving the decimal does not change the value of the quotient, when both decimals are moved the same number of places.

Divide: 57 ÷ 25.

$$25\overline{)575} \quad \frac{2}{}$$

Multiply: 2 × 25.
Subtract: 57 − 50.

$$\begin{array}{r} 2 \\ 25\overline{)575} \\ 50 \\ \hline 7 \end{array}$$

Bring down the 5 from the divisor.

$$\begin{array}{r} 2 \\ 25\overline{)575} \\ 50\downarrow \\ \hline 75 \end{array}$$

> For dividends that still have decimal places after moving the decimal point, place the decimal point on the division box, directly above the decimal in the dividend.
>
> $$0.25\overline{)575.0}$$

Repeat the steps.

$$\begin{array}{r} 23 \\ 25\overline{)575} \\ 50 \\ \hline 75 \\ 75 \\ \hline 0 \end{array}$$

Olina sold 23 cups of lemonade on her first day.

> Because multiplication is the inverse, or opposite, of division, it can be used to check your answer by "undoing" it.

Think About It

If a dividend has two decimal places and the divisor has one decimal place, how many places will the dividend have after converting the divisor to a whole number? Give an example to show your reasoning.

_____

_____

_____

 Focused Instruction

You may work with decimals in formulas. Be sure you know the formula you need and how to use it. Look at the figure below. Work with a partner to answer the questions.

➤ A mailing label is shown below.

2.4 inches

Joyce Ober
520 East Bainbridge St
Elizabethtown, PA 17022

> The area formula is:
> *Area = length × width.*

The area of the label is 3.36 square inches, and the length is 2.4 inches.

What operation do you use to find area? _____

You have the area and the length, so what operation can you use to find the width of the label?

_____

Which number is the dividend? _____

Which number is the divisor? _____

How many decimal places will the decimal move in the

divisor? _____ In the dividend? _____

> When you move the decimal point in a number, you are multiplying by a power of 10.

Where will you place the decimal point on top of the division box?

_____

What is the divisor after moving the decimal point?

_____

What is the dividend after moving the decimal point?

_____

In the space at the right, find the quotient using vertical division.

What is the quotient of 3.36 and 2.4? _____

What is the width of the label in inches?

_____

Be sure to correctly identify the divisor and the dividend in a word problem.

➤ A ride on a wooden roller coaster at a theme park is about 2.58 minutes long. A ride on a metal roller coaster is 1.2 minutes long. How many times longer is the ride on the wooden roller coaster than on the metal roller coaster?

Which number is the dividend? _____

Which number is the divisor? _____

How many places will the decimal point move in the divisor?

_____

What is the divisor after moving the decimal point? _____

How many places will the decimal point move in the dividend? _____

What is the dividend after moving the decimal point? _____

In the space at the right complete the division using vertical division.

How many times longer is the ride on the wooden roller coaster than on the metal roller coaster? _____

> The divisor is the number doing the dividing.

> Remember to add trailing 0s to the dividend to continue dividing.

Use what you know about dividing decimals to find these quotients.

1   $14.25 \div 1.9 =$ _____

2   $5.04 \div 0.8 =$ _____

3   $12.22 \div 4.7 =$ _____

4   $24.48 \div 7.2 =$ _____

Solve the following problems.

1 A kilogram is equal to 2.2 pounds. A large opossum weighs
13.86 pounds. What is the opossum's weight in kilograms?
Show your work.

> The decimal point
> moves the same
> number of places
> in both numbers.

Answer _____ kilograms

2 A soccer field is 95.55 meters long. One yard is about 0.91 meter.
What is the length of the soccer field in yards? Show your work.

> You may bring
> down more than
> one number.

Answer _____ yards

3 A grocery store is having a sale on peanut butter. The cost of peanut
butter before the sale was $2.40 per jar. The cost before the sale was
1.5 times the sale price. What is the sale price of the peanut butter?
Explain how you found your answer.

> Remember to
> place the decimal
> point above the
> division box.

_____

_____

_____

Solve the following problems.

1 What is the quotient of 0.36 ÷ 9?

    A 0.04

    B 0.4

    C 3.24

    D 4.0

2 The price of plantains is $0.89 per pound. Kara spends $4.45 on plantains. How many pounds of plantains did Kara buy? Show your work.

Answer _____ pounds

3 Paolo is putting carpet in his daughter's bedroom. A diagram of the floor is shown below.

10.5 ft

Part A The area of the bedroom floor is 176.4 square feet. What is the length of the bedroom? Show your work.

Answer _____ feet

Part B How many times greater is the length than the width?

Answer _____

Explain how you found your answer.

_____

_____

_____

4 Which expressions have a value of 0.2? Select the **three** correct answers.

    A 0.13 ÷ 6.5

    B 0.38 ÷ 1.9

    C 2.68 ÷ 1.34

    D 2.4 ÷ 12.0

    E 1.8 ÷ 9

    F 0.36 ÷ 18

5 In 2013, Cool Game Corporation made a profit of $84.7 million. The profit made in 2013 was 2.2 times the profit the company made in 2012.

    Part A What was Cool Game Corporation's profit in 2012? Show your work.

        Answer $_____ million

    Part B Explain why you can move the decimal point in the divisor to the right as long as you also move the decimal point in the dividend the same number of places to the right.

_____

_____

_____

_____

6 A state park gift shop sells 3 postcards for $1.95. What is the cost of one postcard? Show your work.

Answer $_____

7 The table below shows the approximate length of some of the shortest rivers in the world.

River	Aril	Comal	Correntoso
Length (in miles)	0.109	2.5	0.124

Complete each statement by filling in the blanks. Find your answers to the tenths.

The Comal River is about _____ times longer than the Aril River. The

difference between how many times longer the Comal is than the Correntoso

and how many times longer the Comal is than the Aril is about _____.

Number and Operations in Base Ten

Solve the following problems.

1   Jaime and his parents are driving to visit their family. They will drive
for 2 days to get there.

Part A   Jaime's parents average about 60 miles per hour on the first
day. If they drive for 9 hours before stopping, how far did
they drive on the first day? Show your work.

Answer _____miles

Part B   The average speed during their second day of travel is
1.1 times greater than the first day. Write an expression that
can be used to find their average speed on the second day.

Answer _____

Part C   If Jaime's parents drove 528 miles on the second day, how
many hours did they drive? Explain how you found your
answer.

_____

_____

_____

2 Use the clues in the information below to find the missing numbers.

19□□

The year that the first man walked on the moon has some digits missing. The tens digit is 3 less than the digit in the hundreds place. The digit in the hundreds place has a place value that is 100 times greater than the digit in the ones place. What year did the first man walk on the moon?

Answer _____

3 Complete the table below by identifying the number of decimal places the decimal will move and in what direction, when solving the expression.

Expression	Number of Places Decimal Point Moved	Direction Decimal Point Moved (left or right)
2.308×10^4		
0.615×10^7		
$47.304 \div 10^5$		

4 What is the expanded form of the decimal 0.64?

A $(6 \times \frac{1}{10}) + (4 \times \frac{1}{100})$

B $(6 \times \frac{1}{100}) + (4 \times \frac{1}{10})$

C $(6 \times \frac{1}{100}) + (4 \times \frac{1}{100})$

D $(6 \times 1) + (4 \times \frac{1}{10})$

5 When multiplying a decimal by a power of 10, the decimal moves. Explain why this happens, using words or numbers.

_____

_____

_____

_____

6 Which comparison statements are correct? Select the **three** correct answers.

A $(1 \times 10) + (7 \times 1) + \left(4 \times \frac{1}{100}\right) > (2 \times 1) + \left(8 \times \frac{1}{10}\right) + \left(1 \times \frac{1}{100}\right)$

B $(1 \times 10) + (7 \times 1) + \left(4 \times \frac{1}{100}\right) > (2 \times 10) + (8 \times 1) + \left(1 \times \frac{1}{10}\right)$

C $(1 \times 100) + (7 \times 10) + (4 \times 10) < (2 \times 10) + (8 \times 1) + \left(1 \times \frac{1}{10}\right)$

D $(1 \times 1) + \left(7 \times \frac{1}{10}\right) > \left(2 \times \frac{1}{10}\right) + \left(8 \times \frac{1}{100}\right)$

E $\left(1 \times \frac{1}{10}\right) + \left(7 \times \frac{1}{100}\right) < (2 \times 1) + \left(8 \times \frac{1}{10}\right) + \left(1 \times \frac{1}{100}\right)$

F $\left(1 \times \frac{1}{10}\right) + \left(7 \times \frac{1}{100}\right) > \left(2 \times \frac{1}{10}\right) + \left(8 \times \frac{1}{100}\right)$

7 During ski season, a ski shop rents sets of skis and poles. The shop rents each set for $39.90. The ski shop rented sets to 481 people one season. How much did the ski shop make on set rentals in this season, after rounding the cost per set to the nearest whole number?

Answer $_____

8 A real estate developer buys three vacant lots next to each other. One lot is 27.5 meters wide, the next lot is 48 meters wide, and the last lot is 33.75 meters wide. If the developer combines the lots, how wide will the combined lot be? Show your work.

Answer _____ meters

9 Mori just replaced the showerhead in her bathroom. The old one used 5.75 gallons per minute (gpm) of water. Her new showerhead uses 2.5 gpm.

Part A How many times as much water did Mori's old showerhead use?

Answer _____ gallons per minute

Part B Explain how you found your answer.

_____

_____

10 Enrico's paycheck for last week was $663. He is paid $17 an hour. How many hours did Enrico work last week?

Answer _____ hours

Operations and Algebraic Thinking

In grade 4, you learned how to recognize patterns and practiced multiplication and division of whole numbers. Now you can use what you know about patterns and the order of operations to write and solve numerical expressions with multiple operations, and turn patterns into input-output tables and graphs.

LESSON 15 Understanding and Writing Expressions In this lesson, you will write numerical expressions, follow the order of operations, and match numerical expressions to their equivalent statements.

LESSON 16 Evaluating Expressions In this lesson, you will evaluate numerical expressions by reading an expression as a set of instructions and following the order of operations to solve for the value of expressions with multiple operations.

LESSON 17 Patterns and Relationships In this lesson, you will recognize the rules of patterns, use input-output tables to graph data on a coordinate plane, and write values as ordered pairs.

LESSON 15 Understanding and Writing Expressions

Introduction

An **expression** is a grouping of numbers, symbols, and operations that shows the value of something. Expressions can be used to write a sentence written in words, numbers, and symbols.

10 more than 15	8 times 2	20 divided by 4	the difference of 19 and 13
15 + 10	8 × 2	20 ÷ 4	19 − 13

The order in which numbers occur in a written sentence may not always be the way they are written in a numerical expression. For addition and multiplication, the order does not change the value. For subtraction and division, the order does change the value.

> The commutative property says that numbers can be added or multiplied in any order.

3 less than 9	the quotient of 9 and 3	the sum of 9 and 3	3 times 9
9 − 3	9 ÷ 3	9 + 3	3 × 9
not	not	or	or
3 − 9	3 ÷ 9	3 + 9	9 × 3

When writing expressions, use key words to order and figure out operations to use.

Addition	Subtraction	Multiplication	Division
the sum	the difference	the product of	the quotient
plus	minus	times	divided by
added to	less than	double/triple	equally
more/greater	fewer	$\frac{1}{2}$ of, $\frac{1}{4}$ of, etc.	separate
increased	decreased by	factor of	per
altogether	remain	at this rate	
combined	how many left		

Parentheses ( ) and brackets [ ] in expressions are used to show a grouping within the expression. Always do operations inside grouping symbols first.

> When there is more than one grouping symbol, work from the inside out.

the sum of 4 and 3 minus 5

the product of 2 and the sum of 1 and 7, plus 6

(4 + 3) − 5

[2 × (1 + 7)] + 6

Kenai is 3 years older than 2 times his sister's age. His sister is 5 years old. Write Kenai's age as a numerical expression.

Kenai is 2 times his sister's age of 5 years: 2×5.

Kenai is also 3 years older than the product. Use parentheses: $(2 \times 5) + 3$.

Think About It

Describe why it is important that numbers are grouped and calculated in a specific order. Give an example to model your explanation.

_____

_____

_____

② Focused Instruction

Always think about the order of the operations. Look for key words. Work with a partner to answer the questions.

➤ A Labrador retriever weighs 10 pounds less than 3 times the weight of a large beagle. The beagle weighs 28 pounds. Write a numerical expression that can be used to find the weight of the Labrador retriever.

What is the weight of the beagle? _____

What operation is indicated by "3 times the weight"?

_____

What operation is indicated by "10 pounds less"?

_____

Which operation must be done first?

_____

Write the part of the expression that must be done first.

_____

> Will you need to do one step before another? How can you group numbers together?

How can you indicate that this part must be done first?

_____

Is the 10 pounds taken from 3 times the weight, or is 3 times the weight taken from the 10 pounds?

_____

Write the numerical expression that can be used to find the weight of the

Labrador retriever. _____

_____

➤ Stella walked to the park on the short path. This path is 108 yards long. She took the long path home, which is twice as long as the short path. Write an expression that can be used to find the total distance Stella walked.

> Look for key words in the problem that tell you about operations.

What is the distance of the shorter

path? _____

What operation do the words "twice as long" indicate?

_____

What number does the word "twice" mean? _____

How can you group this part of the expression?

_____

Write an expression that can be used to find the length of the long path.

_____

What operation does the word "total" indicate?

_____

How do you find the total?

_____

Write a numerical expression that can be used to find the total distance that

Stella walked. _____

Use what you know about key words and operations to write the numerical expressions described below.

1 the quotient of 8 and 2 _____

2 5 less than 12 _____

3 the product of 10 and 15 _____

4 the sum of the product of 2 and 13 and the product of 8 and 7

_____

5 the difference of 33 and the sum of 11 and 6

_____

6 the sum of 14 and the product of 6 and 9

_____

Solve the following problems.

1 Shannon and Daria donated their hair to a charity. Shannon donated 5 inches more than one-third of the length Daria donated. Daria donated 9 inches of hair. Write an expression that can be used to find the amount of hair Shannon donated.

> To multiply unit fractions, you can also divide by the denominator.

Answer _____

2 A poster company is printing an enlarged poster from an original it had in stock. The enlarged poster has a width that is 6 times greater than 2 plus the width of the original. The width of the original is 24 inches. Write an expression that can be used to find the width of the enlarged poster.

> What value do you multiply by 6?

Answer _____

3 The drawing shows the number of babies in the hospital nursery on Monday morning. One-half of the babies are girls. That day 3 more baby girls are born and no boys.

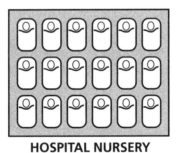

HOSPITAL NURSERY

> Count the number of babies in the nursery first.

Part A If no babies leave the hospital, what expression can you use to find the number of baby girls in the nursery on Monday night?

Answer _____

Part B Explain how you found your answer.

_____

_____

_____

Solve the following problems.

1   René is putting up rain gutters on his house. One piece of the rain gutter measures 48 inches long. A longer piece of gutter is 12 inches shorter than 2 times the length of the shorter gutter. Write an expression that can be used to find the length of the longer gutter.

Answer _____

2   Jerome is 7 years old. His cousin Deion is 4 years younger than 3 times Jerome's age. Which expression can be used to find Deion's age?

A $(7 \times 4) - 3$

B $(7 \times 3) - 4$

C $7 \times (3 - 4)$

D $7 \times (4 - 3)$

3   Chloe found 8 chocolate coins during a scavenger hunt. Her brother Hwa found $\frac{1}{4}$ of the number of coins as their friend David. David found 4 more coins than Chloe.

Part A   Write an expression that can be used to find the number of coins that Hwa found.

Answer _____

Part B   Explain how you found your answer.

_____

_____

_____

_____

_____

4 Amon scored an 86 after playing one game of bowling. Leena's score was 18 less than twice Trevin's score. Trevin scored 6 points less than Amon. Write an expression that can be used to find the number of points Leena scored.

Answer _____

5 How does the expression $7 \times (6 + 5)$ compare to the expression $6 + 5$? Explain how you know.

_____

_____

_____

6 The weight of 1 cubic foot of seawater is about 64 pounds. The weight of 1 cubic foot of cast iron is 7 times greater than seawater. Write an expression that can be used to find the weight of 1 cubic foot of cast iron.

Answer _____

7 Match each expression in the box with the correct statement.

32 less than the sum of 26 and 15 _____	**a.** $32 - (26 + 15)$
the difference of 32 and the sum of 26 and 15 _____	**b.** $15 + (26 + 32)$
15 greater than the difference of 32 and 26 _____	**c.** $(15 + 32) + 26$
15 more than the sum of 26 and 32 _____	**d.** $(26 + 15) - 32$
the sum of 15 and 32 increased by 26 _____	**e.** $15 + (32 - 26)$

8 Claudio and Vera are playing a game where they answer questions and earn points. Claudio answers 16 easy questions that are worth 1 point each. Vera answers 7 fewer questions than Claudio. Vera's questions are worth double Claudio's because they are harder. Write an expression you can use to find how many points Vera and Claudio earned altogether.

Answer _____

1 Introduction

When you **evaluate** a numerical expression, you find the value of the expression. You can use the expression like a set of instructions for finding its equivalent value.

Maria plays a tennis set in which she scores a total of 21 points. If she scores a total of 15 points before taking a break, how many points did she score after the break?

First, write an expression to find the number of points she scored after the break: $21 - 15$. Then, evaluate the expression: $21 - 15 = 6$ points scored after the break.

Parentheses are used to group numbers and operations that need to be done first in a problem that has more than one operation.

> **Equations** show that two expressions are equal. Use an equals sign to separate the expressions.
>
> $21 - 5 = 6$

Maria wins 4 games in a tennis set. She wins the first 3 games with 5 points each. She wins the fourth game with 1 more point than she scored in 1 of the first 3 games. How many points did she score altogether?

Write an expression to show the total score after 4 games. The key word in the problem is *each,* which means multiplication. So the first 3 games had a score of 3×5. The fourth game has a score that is 1 more than the points she scored in one of the first 3 games, so $5 + 1$. To find the points she scored altogether, add the two parts of the expression together, 3×5 and $5 + 1$, using parentheses. Then evaluate using the order of operations.

$$(5 \times 3) + (5 + 1) =$$
$$(15) + (6) = 21$$

Maria scored 21 points altogether.

When addition and subtraction are in the same part of an expression, work from left to right. Likewise, when multiplication and division are in the same expression, work from left to right.

> The **order of operations** explains in which order operations should be done:
> 1. Parentheses/Brackets
> 2. Exponents
> 3. Multiply and divide from left to right
> 4. Add and subtract from left to right

$$4 - 1 + 3 =$$
$$3 + 3 = 6$$

$$6 \times 6 \div 3 =$$
$$36 \div 3 = 12$$

Think About It 💭

Why do you think parentheses are important when you are writing and solving expressions?

_____

_____

2 Focused Instruction

Think about the correct order of operations when you are evaluating expressions.

➤ Look at this expression.

$$[16 - (3 \times 5) + 8] \div 3$$

Which symbol indicates the first step in evaluating the expression?

_____

Which step should be done first?

_____

What is the value of that part of the expression? _____

Which symbol indicates the next step in evaluating the expression?

_____

Which step should be done next?

_____

What is the value of that part of the expression? _____

Which step should be done third?

_____

What is the value of that part of the expression? _____

What is the final step in evaluating the expression?

_____

What is the value of the expression? _____

> Brackets and parentheses are both grouping symbols. When both are in an expression, do the inside one first.

A table can help you plot the steps you need to take to find the solution to an expression.

➤ Look at this expression.

$$34 + 17 \times 2 - 8 + [6 - (5 - 4)]$$

Complete the table. Describe the correct order in which to calculate each operation and how to do it. The first step in the evaluation is given in the table.

Step	Operation	Reasoning
1	(5 − 4)	Parentheses indicate the part that should be completed first.
2	[6 − (1)]	
3		Order of operations states that multiplication should be done before addition and subtraction.
4		
5		
6		

What is the value of the expression? _____

Use what you know about order of operations to evaluate these expressions.

1 $(9 + 11) + (40 - 23) =$ _____

2 $[7 \times (16 - 8) + 7] \div 9 =$ _____

3 $101 + 57 - 10 \times 5 =$ _____

Solve the following problems.

1 What is the value of the expression $(29 - 12) \times 2 - 15$? Show your work.

> Use the letters PEMDAS to remember the order of operations.

Answer _____

2 Jovan evaluated the expression $[9 + (6 \times 3) \div 9] - 1$ as shown below.

> If brackets and parentheses appear in an expression, which should you do first?

$$[9 + (6 \times 3) \div 9] - 1 = [9 + (18) \div 9] - 1$$
$$= [27 \div 9] - 1$$
$$= [3] - 1$$
$$= 2$$

Part A What error did Jovan make in evaluating the expression?

_____

Part B What is the correct value of the expression? Show your work.

Answer _____

3 Evaluate the expression. Show your work.

$$34 - 12 \div 6 + 11$$

> What is the first step if there are no parentheses?

Answer _____

Solve the following problems.

1 Which of the following expressions have a value of 27? Select the **three** correct answers.

A $28 + (18 + 6) \div 2$

B $(12 \times 2) + 3$

C $[3 \times (6 + 7)] - (2 \times 6)$

D $5 + 20 \div 5 \times 4 + 7$

E $50 \div 10 + 3 + (7 \times 2)$

F $(21 \div 7) + \frac{1}{2} \times (9 \times 4) + 6$

2 Look at the expression below.

$$55 \div 11 + [7 \times (2 + 3)] - (40 \div 4)$$

The first two steps to evaluate the expression are partially completed.
Complete the first two steps and write the remaining steps on the blank lines.

$55 \div 11 + [7 \times (2 + 3)] - (40 \div 4) = 55 \div 11 + [7 \times (\underline{\hspace{2cm}})] - (40 \div 4)$

$= 55 \div 11 + [\underline{\hspace{2cm}}] - (40 \div 4)$

$= \underline{\hspace{4cm}}$

$= \underline{\hspace{4cm}}$

$= \underline{\hspace{4cm}}$

$= \underline{\hspace{2cm}}$

3 What is the value of the expression? Show your work.

$$8 + 59 - 13 \times (1 + 4)$$

Answer _____

4 Hedy simplifies the expression and explains that it has a value of 4.

$$\frac{1}{4} \times (16 - 4) + 4$$

What order of operations error could Hedy have made? Explain how you know.

_____

_____

_____

5 Mark True or False for each of the following statements.

	True	False
$20 - 5 \times 3$ has a value of 45.	☐	☐
$18 \div [(14 - 12) + 7]$ has a value of 2.	☐	☐
$[46 - (21 \div 3)] - 38$ has a value of 1.	☐	☐

6 Look at the statement below.

$3 \times 10 + 2 \times 5$ has the same value as $3 \times (10 + 2) \times 5$.

Is this statement correct? Why or why not.

_____

_____

_____

_____

7 The expression below is missing a number.

$$(100 \div 20) + (\square \div 6) - 10$$

What number could be used in the box so that the value of the expression is 0?

Answer _____

8 Evaluate this expression. Show your work.

$$45 \div (3 + 6) \times 5 - 8$$

Answer _____

LESSON 17   Patterns and Relationships

2CCSS: 5.OA.3

1 Introduction

A **pattern** is a series of numbers that follow a given rule. Some patterns have two sets of data, one that the rule is applied to, the **input,** and one that is the result of that operation, the **output.** These types of patterns can be organized using **input-output tables** to show this information.

Rule: Add 4

Input	0	1	2	3
Output	4	5	6	7

For this pattern, 4 is added to each input value and the sum is the output value: $0 + 4 = 4$; $1 + 4 = 5$; $2 + 4 = 6$; and $3 + 4 = 7$. The rule remains the same for each input-output pair.

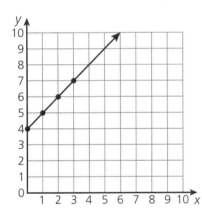

Data from input-output tables can also be graphed on a **coordinate plane.** Each pair of input and output values is written as an **ordered pair.** The input value of each pair is the x-value, while the output value of each pair is the y-value.

The data points shown on the graph correspond to the data in the input table: $(0, 4)$ $(1, 5)$ $(2, 6)$ $(3, 7)$.

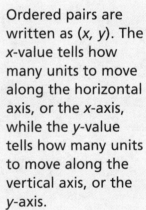

Ordered pairs are written as (x, y). The x-value tells how many units to move along the horizontal axis, or the x-axis, while the y-value tells how many units to move along the vertical axis, or the y-axis.

Compare the input-output data from two patterns using a graph. The input-output table shows a second pattern.

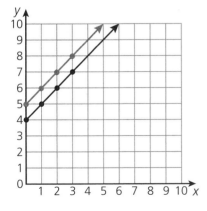

Input	0	1	2	3
Output	5	6	7	8

The second pattern, shown in green, follows the rule of "add 5."

If you compare both patterns, by the rule and by the ordered pairs, you can see that the output values of the second pattern are 1 greater than the corresponding output values of the first pattern.

Think About It

A pattern has a rule that is twice the rule of another pattern. Are the input and output values for the pattern twice the input and output values of the other pattern? Explain your answer.

_____

_____

_____

2 Focused Instruction

Use an input-output table to find the rule. When you find a rule, you can use the rule to find an input or an output number.

➤ The tables below show the number of vegetables in a given number of bunches at a farm stand.

BEETS

Bunches	1	2	3	4
Total Number of Beets	6	12	18	24

CARROTS

Bunches	1	2	3	4
Total Number of Carrots	12	24	36	48

What operations can be used to find the number of beets in 1 bunch of

beets? _____

Which of the operations can also be used to find the number of beets in

2 bunches? _____

Does this rule apply to the other data pairs? _____

What is the rule for the pattern of beets per bunch?

_____

> The rule for an input-output table must apply to all the input-output pairs in the table.

What operations can be used to find the number of carrots in

1 bunch? _____

Which of the operations can also be used to find the number of carrots in

2 bunches? _____

Does this rule apply to the other data pairs? _____

What is the rule for the pattern of carrots per bunch?

_____

If you want 84 carrots, what operation can you use to find the number of bunches you will need?

_____

Write an expression to use to find the number of carrot bunches.

_____

How many bunches will you need? _____

What is the relationship between the two pattern rules?

_____

_____

> Use inverse operations to work backward to find an input or an output.

Input-output pairs are also ordered pairs when you graph the relationship on a coordinate plane. The input is the *x*-value and the output is the *y*-value.

Input	0	1	2	3
Output	3	4	5	6

Input	2	3	5	7
Output	3	4	6	8

Which ordered pair from the first table should be graphed first? _____

Describe how to graph the ordered pair.

_____

_____

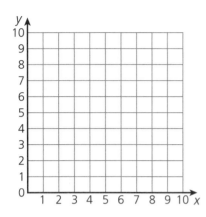

Graph each of the points from the first table on the graph and connect them with a line.

Which ordered pair from the second table should be graphed first? _____

Graph the rest of the points from the second table and connect them with a line. Compare the patterns.

What do you notice about the graphed patterns?

_____

_____

Use what you know about patterns to answer these questions.

1 What is the rule for the pattern shown in the table?

Input	12	11	10	9
Output	6	5	4	3

_____

2 What is the relationship between the rules from the two tables shown here?

Input	4	6	8	10
Output	16	24	32	40

Input	4	6	8	10
Output	2	3	4	5

_____

_____

Solve the following problems.

1 Rockville's and Keytown's Little League teams use the input-output tables below. The input values are the number of players that sign up. The output values are the number of teams they can make. How many teams can be made for each league if 108 players sign up?

Rockville Little League

Input	Output
36	4
45	5
54	6
63	7

Keytown Little League

Input	Output
36	3
48	4
60	5
72	6

Find the rule for each pattern and then extend it to 108 players.

Rockville _____ teams

Keytown _____ teams

2 Look at the tables below.

PATTERN A

Input	Output
0	15
2	17
4	19
5	20

PATTERN B

Input	Output
20	5
19	4
17	2
15	0

Graph the patterns from each of the tables on the coordinate plane below. Label each graph.

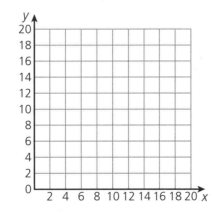

Graph the input along the x-axis and the output along the y-axis.

Solve the following problems.

1 A baker is making muffins. Each pan holds 12 muffins.

Part A Write the rule for the input-output table. Then create an input-output table, using 1, 2, 3, 4, and 6 pans as your input values.

Answer _____

Input	Output

Part B The baker also makes mini-muffins in pans that hold 24. Make an input-output table, using the same input values as Part A. Graph the results of both tables on the same graph. Label the lines.

Input	Output

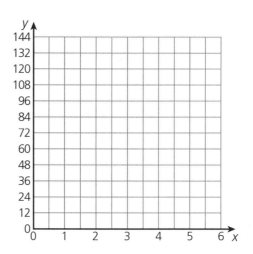

What do you notice about the numbers of muffins and mini-muffins?

Answer _____

2 During gym class, students play a jumping game. Each student starts 0.5 foot
from the gym wall and takes 10 jumps. The total distances after different
numbers of jumps for two students are shown on the tables below.

Jordan

Jumps	1	2	4	5
Distance (feet)	1.5	2.5	4.5	5.5

Greg

Jumps	1	3	5	7
Distance (feet)	2	5	8	11

If the jumps continue to increase by the same amounts, how much farther
will Greg have jumped than Jordan by the tenth jump?

Answer _____ feet

Explain how you know.

_____

_____

_____

3 Look at the graph below.

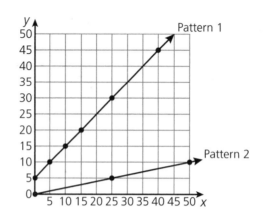

What are the rules of the patterns shown by the graph?

A   Pattern 1: multiply by 5, Pattern 2: add 25

B   Pattern 1: add 5, Pattern 2: multiply by 5

C   Pattern 1: add 5, Pattern 2: divide by 5

D   Pattern 1: multiply by 5, Pattern 2: subtract 20

4 Complete the input-output tables below.

Input	2	4		8
Output	9	11	13	

Input	8	6		1
Output	7	5	3	

5 Following the rule, which pairs of values belong in the table? Select the **two** correct answers.

Input	20	16	12	8
Output	5	4	3	2

A (1, 4)

B (4, 1)

C (4, 2)

D (2, 1)

E (24, 6)

F (6, 24)

G (8, 24)

H (24, 8)

Solve the following problems.

1 There are 72 passengers on a subway train. At the next stop, the train picks up 15 more passengers. By the tenth station, the train has double the number of passengers than were on the train after the second station. Write an expression that is equal to the number of passengers on the train at the tenth station.

Answer _____

2 Which expressions have a value of 3? Select the **two** correct answers.

A $(4 + 2) \div 3 \times 1$

B $4 - 2 \times 1 + 1$

C $1 + 3 \times 2 - 5$

D $4 + 3 - 2 \times 2$

E $(6 \div 2) \times (1 \times 0)$

F $(5 + 3) \div 2$

3 A park has 39 visitors on Friday. The number of visitors on Saturday is 5 times that, plus 12. Write an expression you could use to find the number of visitors to the park on Saturday.

Answer _____

4 The graph below shows two patterns.

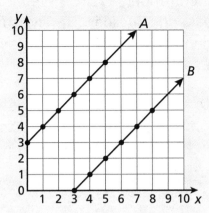

Part A What are the rules of each of the patterns?

Answer _____

Part B What is the relationship between the outputs of the
patterns? Explain how you know.

_____

_____

_____

5 Look at the two expressions.

Expression 1	**Expression 2**
50 × 7 + (11 − 6)	50 × (7 + 11) − 6

Circle an option in each set that makes the following statement true.

The value of [Expression 1, Expression 2] is [1,750, 894, 539, 355]
greater than the value of the other expression.

6 On Monday, one share of stock in a computer company cost $58. On Tuesday, the value of a share dropped $32. On Wednesday, the value of a share was 4 times its value on Tuesday. On Thursday, the value of a share was $19 less than on Wednesday. On Friday, the value of a share was one-fifth of what it was on Thursday.

Part A Write and evaluate an expression to find the value of the stock on Wednesday. Then use your answer to write and evaluate an expression to find the value of the stock on Friday.

Wednesday _____

Friday _____

Part B Mr. Kwon owns some shares of this stock. He wants to sell it on the day it has the greatest worth so he will make the greatest profit. On what day should Mr. Kwon sell his stock? Explain your answer.

_____

_____

_____

_____

7 Which words or phrases indicate that multiplication should be used? Select the **three** correct answers.

A   times

B   altogether

C   product of

D   remaining

E   equally

F   at this rate

8 A sheet of stamps has 20 stamps on it. A roll of stamps contains 100 stamps.

Part A Complete the tables using the patterns for each.

Sheets	Stamps
1	20
2	
3	
5	
8	
10	
12	

Rolls	Stamps
1	100
2	
3	
5	
8	
10	
12	

Part B For what inputs are the outputs of these tables equal?

Answer _____

9 Arya is the star batter for her softball team. At the beginning of the season, she hits an average of 18 balls during batting practice. At the end of the season, she hits twice that number decreased by 8.

Part A Write an expression that can be used to find the number of balls she hits during batting practice at the end of the season.

Answer _____

Part B What is the average number of balls Arya hits during batting practice at the end of the season?

Answer _____ balls

10 A youth group is going camping. Their tents hold 6 people each. They are traveling in vans that hold 10 people each.

Part A Complete the input-output tables if the input values are the numbers of tents or vans and the output values are the numbers of campers.

TENTS

Input	Output
1	
2	
3	
5	
10	

VANS

Input	Output
1	
2	
3	
5	
10	

Part B Graph lines to show these relationships on the coordinate plane below. Label each graph.

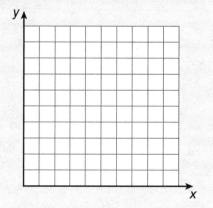

In grade 4, you learned how to compare and multiply fractions, and in Unit 3, you reviewed multiplication and division. Now you can use what you know about fractions to perform operations with fractions.

LESSON 18 Adding and Subtracting Fractions with Unlike Denominators In this lesson, you will add and subtract fractions with unlike denominators by converting them to fractions with like denominators.

LESSON 19 Word Problems with Addition and Subtraction of Fractions In this lesson, you will add and subtract fractions to solve word problems.

LESSON 20 Connecting Fractions and Division In this lesson, you will write each division expression as a fraction in lowest terms, write remainders, and use division models and equations to understand problems.

LESSON 21 Multiplying Whole Numbers and Fractions In this lesson, you will write multiplication or division expressions to work with fractions and whole numbers. You will write answers as proper fractions in their lowest terms or as mixed numbers.

LESSON 22 Multiplying Fractions In this lesson, you will convert mixed numbers and improper fractions, multiply fractions, and express products in lowest terms.

LESSON 23 Multiplication and Scale In this lesson, you will predict the size of products using values of fractions. You will draw diagrams, write comparison symbols to make statements true, and consider whether fractions are greater or less than 1.

LESSON 24 Word Problems with Multiplication of Fractions In this lesson, you will multiply fractions and mixed numbers to solve word problems, convert fractions, use common divisors, and find the products.

LESSON 25 Dividing with Unit Fractions In this lesson, you will use reciprocals to divide by fractions. You will model expressions with pictures, multiply by reciprocals, and write expressions and quotients.

LESSON 26 Word Problems with Division and Fractions In this lesson, you will practice multiplying by the reciprocal of a fraction. You will write division and multiplication expressions and identify dividends, divisors, and quotients.

LESSON 18 Adding and Subtracting Fractions with Unlike Denominators

1 Introduction

Fractions describe part of a whole. **Equivalent fractions** have the same value. To add or subtract fractions, the denominators must be the same. Rewrite fractions with unlike denominators by finding equivalent fractions with the same denominator.

To write equivalent fractions, you can find the **least common denominator (LCD).** This is the same as the least common multiple (LCM) of the two denominators.

To add or subtract fractions, add or subtract the numerators. The denominator stays the same.

What is the sum of $\frac{1}{4} + \frac{2}{3}$?

> To write equivalent fractions with the same denominator, you can also multiply the numerator and denominator of one fraction by the denominator of the other fraction.

Find equivalent fractions with common denominators.

$$\frac{1}{4} \times \frac{3}{3} = \frac{3}{12} \qquad \frac{2}{3} \times \frac{4}{4} = \frac{8}{12}$$

Then add the numerators. Write the sum over the common denominator.

$$\frac{3}{12} + \frac{8}{12} = \frac{3+8}{12} = \frac{11}{12}$$

So the sum of $\frac{1}{4} + \frac{2}{3}$ is $\frac{11}{12}$.

A fraction is in **lowest terms** when it cannot be reduced by dividing the numerator and denominator by the same number, or a common divisor.

Subtract $\frac{4}{5} - \frac{3}{10}$.

> Sometimes you will only need to change one of the fractions.

Since 10 is the least common multiple of 5 and 10, the least common denominator is 10. Multiply the numerator and denominator of $\frac{4}{5}$ by 2.

$$\frac{4}{5} \times \frac{2}{2} = \frac{8}{10}$$

Subtract the numerators. Write the difference over the common denominator.

$$\frac{8}{10} - \frac{3}{10} = \frac{8-3}{10}$$

The difference of $\frac{8}{10} - \frac{3}{10}$ is $\frac{5}{10}$. Since both 5 and 10 are divisible by 5, put the fraction in lowest terms by dividing.

$$\frac{5}{10} \div \frac{5}{5} = \frac{1}{2}$$

Whatever you do to the numerator, you must also do to the denominator.

Think About It

Why might it be important to reduce fractions to lowest terms?

_____

_____

2 Focused Instruction

When you find the least common denominator, you make it easier to put the sum or the difference in lowest terms.

➤ What is the sum of $\frac{3}{4} + \frac{1}{6}$?

What is the first step for adding these fractions?

_____

What is the least common multiple of 4 and 6? _____

What is the least common denominator of $\frac{3}{4}$ and $\frac{1}{6}$? _____

By what number should you multiply the numerator and denominator of the fraction $\frac{3}{4}$? _____

What is the equivalent fraction? _____

By what number should you multiply the numerator and denominator of the fraction $\frac{1}{6}$? _____

What is the equivalent fraction? _____

The least common multiple is the smallest multiple that is the same for both denominators.

To add fractions, do you add the numerators? _____ Do you add the

denominators? _____

> To simplify a
> fraction means
> to put it in
> lowest terms.

What is the sum of $\frac{3}{4} + \frac{1}{6}$? _____

Can you simplify the sum anymore? _____

➤ What is the difference between $\frac{9}{12}$ and $\frac{3}{6}$?

Write a subtraction expression that can be used to find the difference.

_____

List the first three multiples for 6. _____

List the first three multiples for 12. _____

What is the least common denominator for 6 and 12? _____

Fill in the boxes in each equation to change the fractions to equivalent
fractions with common denominators.

> The least common
> denominator may
> be one of the given
> denominators.

$$\frac{9}{12} \times \frac{\square}{\square} = \frac{\square}{\square} \qquad \frac{3}{6} \times \frac{\square}{\square} = \frac{\square}{\square}$$

What is the difference of the two fractions? _____

Can the difference be reduced by dividing the numerator and denominator by a

common number? If so, what is the common divisor? _____

What is the difference in lowest terms? _____

Use what you know about adding and subtracting fractions to find these sums and differences. Give your answers in lowest terms.

1 $\dfrac{1}{7} + \dfrac{5}{6} =$ _____

2 $\dfrac{2}{3} + \dfrac{4}{6} =$ _____

3 $\dfrac{3}{11} - \dfrac{1}{9} =$ _____

4 $\dfrac{21}{32} - \dfrac{9}{16} =$ _____

Solve the following problems.

1 Hiram explains that the sum of $\frac{4}{7} + \frac{14}{21}$ has a denominator of 28.

> **Part A** What error did Hiram make when adding the two fractions? Explain how you know.

What is the first step in adding unlike fractions?

_____

_____

_____

> **Part B** What is the correct sum of the fractions?

> **Answer** _____

2 Alice's math homework includes this problem:

$$\frac{6}{9} - \frac{2}{6} = \square$$

Explain how Alice should find the difference.

Solve the problem to help write an explanation of the steps.

_____

_____

_____

_____

3 What is the sum of the fractions below?

$$\frac{1}{8} + \frac{7}{10} = \square$$

Remember to use equivalent fractions to rewrite the problem using like denominators.

Answer _____

Solve the following problems.

1 Find the sum of $\frac{3}{5}$ and $\frac{5}{12}$. Show your work.

Answer _____

2 Mark True or False for each problem.

	True	False
$\frac{8}{9} - \frac{2}{3} = \frac{2}{9}$	☐	☐
$\frac{4}{5} + \frac{1}{7} = \frac{5}{12}$	☐	☐
$\frac{6}{12} - \frac{3}{8} = \frac{3}{72}$	☐	☐
$\frac{6}{4} + \frac{5}{2} = 4$	☐	☐

3 Which of these fractions are equal to the difference of $\frac{4}{3} - \frac{2}{13}$? Select the **two** correct answers.

A $\frac{2}{10}$

B $\frac{46}{39}$

C $\frac{6}{16}$

D $1\frac{7}{39}$

E $\frac{2}{39}$

F $\frac{12}{13}$

4 Franklin solved this problem: $\frac{2}{5} + \frac{3}{7} = \frac{1}{3}$. How can you prove that his answer is incorrect using number sense?

_____

_____

_____

5 What is the difference between the fractions below? Express your answer in lowest terms.

$$\frac{10}{16} - \frac{2}{8} = \square$$

Answer _____

6 Sardo found the solution to $\frac{5}{6} + \frac{9}{10}$.

Part A Fill in the boxes to show how Sardo found the sum of $\frac{5}{6}$ and $\frac{9}{10}$.

$$\frac{5}{6} + \frac{9}{10} = \frac{5 \times \Box}{6 \times \Box} + \frac{9 \times \Box}{10 \times \Box}$$

$$\downarrow$$

$$\frac{\Box}{30} + \frac{27}{\Box} = \frac{\Box}{\Box}$$

Part B What is the sum written in lowest terms?

Answer _____

7 Find the difference.

$$\frac{7}{11} - \frac{1}{2} = \Box$$

Answer _____

Word Problems with Addition and Subtraction of Fractions

 Introduction

To add and subtract fractions, both fractions must have a **common denominator,** or denominator that is the same. You can add and subtract fractions to solve many kinds of problems.

The width of a small paper clip is $\frac{3}{8}$ inch. The width of a large paper clip is $\frac{2}{5}$ inch. What is the combined width of both paper clips?

$$\frac{3}{8} + \frac{2}{5}$$

You must add to find the combined width. Change the fractions to equivalent fractions with common denominators.

To find a common denominator, find the least common multiple (LCM) of the two denominators. The LCM of 8 and 5 is 40.

$$\frac{3 \times 5}{8 \times 5} + \frac{2 \times 8}{5 \times 8} = \frac{15}{40} + \frac{16}{40}$$

> Review how to find equivalent fractions with common denominators in Lesson 18.

Add the numerators of the fractions. Write the sum over the common denominator.

$$\frac{15}{40} + \frac{16}{40} = \frac{31}{40}$$

The combined width of the paper clips is $\frac{31}{40}$ inch.

> When possible, reduce your answer to lowest terms.

Think About It

Explain why both the numerator and denominator of a fraction always need to have the same operation applied to them when making equivalent fractions.

_____

_____

To add or subtract mixed numbers, be sure that the fractions have a common denominator. Add or subtract the fractions. Then add or subtract the whole numbers. You may need to rewrite a whole number as a fraction.

➤ Cas can run $1\frac{1}{4}$ miles in the same time it takes Dakar to run $2\frac{1}{3}$ miles. How much farther can Dakar run than Cas in the same amount of time?

Is the question asking you to find the difference of the distances or the total combined distance?

_____

What operation will find how much farther Dakar can run than Cas?

_____

Write an expression that can be used to find how much farther Dakar can run.

_____

What are the denominators of the fractions? _____

What is the least common multiple of these two numbers? _____

What number must you multiply the denominator of the first fraction

in the expression by to get the LCD? _____

Multiply the numerator and the denominator of the first fraction to change it to

an equivalent fraction with the LCM as the denominator. _____

Does the whole number change when you write the fraction with a different

denominator? _____

What number must you multiply the denominator of the second fraction by to

get the LCD? _____

What is the second mixed number written as an equivalent fraction with the

LCM as the common denominator? _____

Write an expression using the like fractions that can be used to find how much

farther Dakar can run than Cas. _____

> To find the LCM of two numbers, list their multiples until you find the first one they share.

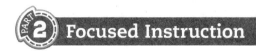

What is the difference of the whole numbers? _____

What is the difference of the fractions? _____

How much farther can Dakar run than Cas in this

time? _____

> If you cannot subtract the second fraction from the first fraction, you can also rename mixed numbers as improper fractions and subtract the numerators.

➤ Cruz and Lindsay are sharing a large sandwich for lunch. Cruz eats $\frac{2}{4}$ of the sandwich and Lindsay eats $\frac{1}{4}$ of the sandwich.

Do the fractions have like denominators? _____

Do the fractions need to be changed in order to find how much of the sandwich

they ate in all? _____

Write an expression that can be used to find the amount of sandwich they ate

altogether. _____

Do you add the numerators? _____ The denominators? _____

How much of the sandwich did Cruz and Lindsay eat altogether? _____

What fraction describes the whole sandwich? _____

Write an expression to show how much of the sandwich was

left. _____

What fraction of the sandwich was left? _____

> A fraction with the same number in the numerator and the denominator is equivalent to 1.

Use what you know about fractions to answer these questions.

Jeremy packed two boxes. One weighed $8\frac{7}{12}$ pounds. The other weighed $12\frac{1}{3}$ pounds.

1   How much more does the second box weigh than the first? _____

2   How much do the two boxes weigh together? _____

Solve the following problems.

1 Fariq has a vase that is $\frac{8}{12}$ foot tall. Xavier has a vase that is $\frac{2}{4}$ foot tall. How much taller is Fariq's vase than Xavier's? Show your work.

> Remember to find a common denominator.

Answer _____ foot

2 Luz's grandmother made a quilt. She had $\frac{11}{18}$ yard of red trim that she sewed to $1\frac{3}{6}$ yards of yellow trim to go around the edge of the quilt. What was the total length of trim Luz's grandmother sewed together? Show your work.

> The word *total* tells you to add.

Answer _____ yards

3 Two rods in a swing set measure $8\frac{5}{16}$ inches and $9\frac{4}{8}$ inches. Alan says the two rods have a difference of $1\frac{1}{16}$ inches. Is Alan correct? Explain your answer.

> You may need to rewrite only one of the fractions.

_____

_____

Solve the following problems.

1   Serena is measuring the lengths of beetles for a science project. One beetle measures $\frac{4}{5}$ centimeter and another measures $\frac{7}{10}$ centimeter. What is the difference in the beetles' lengths? Show your work.

Answer _____ centimeter

2   A breath mint company has a breath mint with a diameter of $\frac{3}{6}$ inch. They want to increase the diameter to make an even larger new mint. They increase the diameter by $\frac{2}{8}$ inch. What is the combined diameter of the small and large mints? Select the **two** correct answers.

A $\frac{8}{20}$ inch

B $\frac{30}{24}$ inches

C $\frac{1}{6}$ inch

D $\frac{18}{24}$ inch

E $\frac{5}{14}$ inch

F $1\frac{1}{4}$ inches

3 Maya finished $2\frac{4}{6}$ books during her winter break. She read $4\frac{1}{2}$ more books during her spring break than her winter break. If she has a total of 12 books to read, how many books does Maya have left to read?

Answer _____ books

Explain how you found your answer.

_____

_____

_____

_____

4 Kelly volunteers at a local animal shelter. She made some notes about the animal populations in the shelter this week.

$\frac{2}{5}$ dogs $\frac{3}{8}$ cats

rest are other pets,
such as birds, hamsters,
and lizards

Part A What fraction of all the animals in the shelter are dogs and cats? What fraction of all the animals are not dogs and cats?

Dogs and Cats _____

Not Dogs and Cats _____

Part B Explain how you found your answers.

_____

_____

_____

5 Thad is $4\frac{1}{6}$ feet tall. If he grows $\frac{1}{4}$ foot in the next year, how tall will Thad be on his next birthday? Show your work.

Answer _____ feet

 **Introduction**

A fraction represents the parts in a whole, but it can also be used to describe division. The fraction bar is also used to show division. A fraction can be read as the numerator being divided by the denominator.

$$\text{fraction or division bar} \rightarrow \frac{1}{2} = 1 \div 2$$

Andy and Carlotta ordered 2 bowls of frozen yogurt to share with 2 of their friends. What part of a whole bowl will each person eat?

$$2 \text{ bowls} \div 4 \text{ people} = \frac{2}{4} \text{ bowl per person}$$

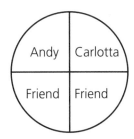 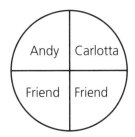

The fraction $\frac{2}{4}$ can be reduced by dividing the numerator and denominator by 2, so $\frac{2 \div 2}{4 \div 2} = \frac{1}{2}$. Each person will get $\frac{1}{2}$ bowl of frozen yogurt.

Think About It

In thinking about fractions as division, how are the parts of a division problem related to the parts of a fraction?

_____

_____

_____

_____

When connecting fractions and division in real-world situations, think about what the answer to the problem represents. Be sure your answer makes sense.

➤ A ball of twine has 60 yards of twine in it. The twine will be split evenly among 8 children at a day camp for a craft project.

Is the twine or the group of children being divided evenly?

_____

Write a division expression, using ÷, which can be used to find the amount of

twine that each child will receive. _____

Which value will be the numerator of the fraction that represents the

division? _____

Which value will be the denominator of the fraction? _____

Write a fraction that can be used to find the length of twine that

each child will receive. _____

How many times will 8 divide into 60 evenly? _____

What is the product of 8 and that number? _____

What is the difference of the product of 8 and 7 and 60? _____

Write the quotient of 60 and 8 as a mixed number. _____

What is the greatest common factor of the numerator and the

denominator? _____

In lowest terms, how much twine will each child get? _____

> Think about the situation. What does a fraction mean in this situation?

➤ A box contains 18 packs of fruit snacks. There are 27 students that are sharing the fruit snacks.

Are the students or the fruit snacks being divided? _____

Write a division expression, using the division symbol, which can be used to find the fraction of a pack of fruit snacks that each student will get.

_____

Which number in the expression is the numerator? _____

Which number in the expression is the denominator? _____

What fraction of a pack of fruit snacks will each student get? _____

What is the greatest number that both the numerator and denominator are divisible by? _____

What is the fraction written in lowest terms? _____

Would it make sense if your quotient was a mixed number? Explain.

_____

_____

> Are there enough packs for each student to have one?

Use what you know about division and fractions to write each problem as a fraction in lowest terms.

1 $5\overline{)45}$ = _____

2 $7 \div 12$ = _____

3 4 loaves of bread shared by 16 people _____

Solve the following problems.

1 A racecar driver drives around a track 20 times. The driver takes 14 minutes to complete all 20 laps. If each lap is completed in the same amount of time, how many minutes does it take to complete 1 lap, in lowest terms?

> Divide the time by laps to find the time per lap.

Answer _____ minute(s)

2 A large jar of paint was separated evenly into 9 smaller containers. The jar contains 237 milliliters of paint. How many milliliters of the paint was in each smaller container? Write your answer as a mixed number.

> Think about which number is the numerator and which is the denominator.

Answer _____ milliliter(s)

3 Ophelia feeds her two cats 13 ounces of cat food each day. Each cat eats an equal amount. She determines that each cat eats $\frac{2}{13}$ ounce each day. What mistake did Ophelia make? Explain how you know.

> Does the answer make sense in the situation? What answer would you expect?

_____

_____

_____

Solve the following problems.

1 Li and her two brothers want to equally share 17 game tokens. How many tokens will each of them get? Ignore the leftover tokens.

A   5

B   6

C $\frac{3}{17}$

D $\frac{17}{3}$

2 Tony is backpacking 94 miles of the Appalachian Trail. Tony hikes the same distance each day for 4 days. Which fraction describes how many miles Tony will travel each day? Select the **two** correct answers.

A $\frac{1}{23}$

B $\frac{2}{47}$

C $20\frac{3}{4}$

D $4\frac{1}{23}$

E $23\frac{1}{2}$

F $\frac{47}{2}$

3 An apple orchard uses 8 crates of apples to make 3 gallons of apple cider. What portion of a crate is used to make a gallon of apple cider?

Answer _____ crate(s)

4 Eva, Beth, and Cara share the work of mowing 7 lawns that are the same size. Each girl mowed exactly the same area. How many lawns did Beth and Cara do together, in lowest terms?

Answer _____ lawns

Explain how you found your answer.

_____

_____

_____

5 Ronaldo makes 4 hats in 5 hours. What portion of a hat does Ronaldo make per hour?

Answer _____ hat

6 The temperature at 7:00 P.M. is 95°F. The temperature increased from 82°F in 6 hours. In the 4 hours before it turned 82°F, the temperature increased from 73°F to 82°F. What was the change in temperature per hour, written as a mixed number?

Answer _____ °F

7 Seth enjoys woodworking and sometimes builds things to sell.

Part A Seth made 5 identical birdhouses in 4 hours. What fraction of an hour did it take Seth to make one birdhouse? Explain why your answer is correct.

_____

_____

_____

_____

Part B Seth made 4 identical shelves in 3 hours. Did it take him more time or less time to make one shelf than one birdhouse? Explain.

_____

_____

_____

Multiplying Whole Numbers and Fractions

 **Introduction**

Use multiplication to find fractions of whole numbers. Models can help you find the answer.

$\frac{1}{2} \times 4 = 2$

The number line shows sections of $\frac{1}{2}$. Four times $\frac{1}{2}$ results in 2 wholes.

Sandwiches cut in half are on a plate. If there are 4 half sandwiches on the plate, how many total sandwiches are there?

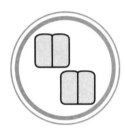

There are $\frac{1}{2} \times 4$ sandwiches, or 2 sandwiches, on the plate.

Whole numbers can also be multiplied by fractions by multiplying the whole number by the numerator and writing the product over the denominator.

$$\frac{1}{2} \times 4 = \frac{1 \times 4}{2} = \frac{4}{2} = 2$$

The fraction bar also shows division. Divide the numerator by the denominator.

Think About It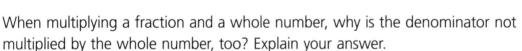

When multiplying a fraction and a whole number, why is the denominator not multiplied by the whole number, too? Explain your answer.

_____

_____

_____

Use diagrams or equations to help you multiply whole numbers and fractions.

➤ There are 52 players on a football team. One-fourth of the players have uniform numbers with the digit 6. How many players on the team have the digit 6 on their uniforms?

> The word *of* usually tells you to multiply.

What does "one-fourth of the players" mean in terms of operations?

_____

Draw a diagram that can be used to show what is happening in the problem, using an X to represent each player.

Write a multiplication expression that can be used to find the number of players

with a 6 on their uniforms. _____

Write a division problem that can be used to find the number of players with a 6

on their uniforms. _____

How many players have the digit 6 on their uniforms? _____

_____

➤ Milena has 20 sheets of fancy paper. She uses $\frac{3}{5}$ of the sheets for a scrapbook.

Draw a model to help you find the number of sheets of fancy paper Milena used. Draw 20 sheets of paper. Divide them into 5 equal groups.

What fraction of the paper did Milena use? _____

How many groups in your model do you need to shade to show this fraction?

_____

Shade this number of groups. How many pieces of paper did you shade?

_____

Fill in the multiplication expression to find the number of sheets of fancy paper Milena used.

Can you cancel common factors to do this multiplication?

_____

Find the value of your multiplication expression. Cancel common factors if possible.

_____

How many pieces of fancy paper did Milena use? _____

> Do the whole number and the denominator have any common factors?

Use what you know about multiplying fractions and whole numbers to find these products.

1 $6 \times \frac{7}{9} =$ _____

2 $10 \times \frac{3}{5} =$ _____

3 $\frac{11}{12} \times 12 =$ _____

Solve the following problems.

1 The top of a dining table is $\frac{7}{2}$ feet by 5 feet. What is the area of the tabletop? Show your work.

> Find the area of a rectangle by multiplying length and width.

Answer _____ square feet

2 There are 4 large water jugs that are set outside a baseball team's dugout. After the fourth inning, $\frac{2}{3}$ of the water in the jugs remains. How many jugs of water are left? Show your work.

> Use an equation or a model to multiply.

Answer _____ jugs

3 A yarn factory makes a small spool of yarn with 90 yards of yarn. A large spool has $2\frac{1}{2}$ times more yarn in a spool. How much yarn does the larger spool have? Show your work.

> Change mixed numbers to improper fractions before multiplying.

Answer _____ yards

Solve the following problems.

1 On a menu, $\frac{1}{10}$ of the 60 dishes are chicken, $\frac{1}{6}$ are beef, $\frac{1}{3}$ are pork, and the rest are vegetarian. If Sergei does not like beef or pork, how many dishes can he choose from on this menu?

   A 30

   B 24

   C 10

   D 6

2 The floor in a kitchen is 16 feet long and $15\frac{1}{2}$ feet wide. It is being retiled. Tiles cover 1 square foot and cost $4 each. How much will it cost to retile the kitchen?

   Answer $_____

3 Mark True or False for each problem.

	True	False
$\frac{2}{9} \times 3 = \frac{6}{9}$	☐	☐
$\frac{8}{5} \times 7 = 10\frac{1}{5}$	☐	☐
$\frac{10}{14} \times 6 = 4\frac{2}{7}$	☐	☐

4 A science class counted 20 bird nests in a park. Out of the total nests, $\frac{2}{5}$ had eggs, and $\frac{3}{10}$ had chicks. The rest of the nests were empty. How many nests were empty?

   Answer _____ nests

5 What is the product of 32 and $\frac{2}{8}$?

Answer _____

6 Dora uses this recipe to make French toast for 12 people.

Recipe for French Toast
(Makes 2 servings)

Ingredients

- 2 eggs
- $\frac{3}{4}$ teaspoon sugar
- $\frac{1}{4}$ teaspoon salt
- $\frac{1}{2}$ cup milk
- 4 slices white bread

Part A Assuming each person will get 1 full serving, how much of each ingredient does Dora need to make enough French toast for everyone? Explain your answer.

_____

_____

_____

_____

Part B If Dora uses the same recipe to make French toast for just herself, how can she find the amount of each ingredient she needs? Explain.

_____

_____

_____

1 Introduction

When multiplying fractions, you can think of finding a smaller portion of a fraction, or a fraction of a fraction.

A sheet of paper is folded into halves. Each $\frac{1}{2}$ is then folded into quarters. On the sheet of paper, $\frac{1}{4}$ of $\frac{1}{2}$ is colored green. What portion of the sheet of paper is green?

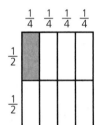

$$\frac{1}{4} \times \frac{1}{2} = \frac{1}{8}$$

On the sheet of paper, $\frac{1}{8}$ is green.

When multiplying fractions, multiply the numerator and denominator of a fraction by the numerator and denominator of the other fraction. Then reduce the fraction to lowest terms.

> Write fractions in lowest terms by dividing the numerator and denominator by the greatest common factor.

$$\frac{4}{6} \times \frac{3}{4} = \frac{4 \times 3}{6 \times 4} = \frac{12}{24} = \frac{1}{2}$$

Fractions that are between 0 and 1 have a product less than both fractions. You can use this to check that your answer is reasonable.

Think About It

If both fractions are greater than 1, is the product greater than both of the fractions? Explain how you found your answer.

_____

_____

_____

Rectangular models can help you understand multiplying fractions.

➤ What is $\frac{3}{8} \times \frac{4}{5}$?

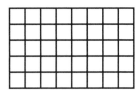

Each column shows $\frac{1}{8}$. Shade columns to show $\frac{3}{8}$.

Each row shows $\frac{1}{5}$. Shade rows to show $\frac{4}{5}$.

How many squares are shaded twice? _____

How many squares are there in all? _____

What is the product of $\frac{3}{8} \times \frac{4}{5}$? _____

What number divides both the numerator and the denominator?

_____

What is the area of the shaded section, in lowest terms? _____

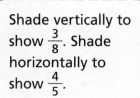

Shade vertically to show $\frac{3}{8}$. Shade horizontally to show $\frac{4}{5}$.

➤ At a farmer's market, $\frac{1}{4}$ of the stands sell homemade jams. Of these stands, $\frac{2}{5}$ also sell homemade bread. What fraction of the stands at the farmer's market sell both homemade jams and bread?

Look at the rectangular model below.

Write the fraction of stands that sell jam on the side of the model. Shade squares to show this fraction.

Write the fraction of stands that sell bread on the top of the model. Shade squares to show this fraction.

Look where the shading overlaps. What fraction of the entire model is this?

_____

Write an expression that can be used to find the fraction of booths that sell both

jam and bread. _____

What is the product of the numerators? _____

What is the product of the denominators? _____

What fraction of the booths sell both jam and bread? _____

What number can both the numerator and the denominator be divided by

to reduce the fraction to lowest terms? _____

What fraction of the booths sell both jam and bread, in lowest terms?

_____

> The general rule for multiplying fractions is
> $$\frac{a}{b} \times \frac{c}{d} = \frac{ac}{bd}$$
> when $b, d \neq 0$.

Use what you know about multiplying fractions to find these products. Give your answers as proper fractions or mixed numbers in lowest terms.

1 $\frac{9}{11} \times \frac{3}{7} =$ _____

2 $\frac{1}{8} \times \frac{10}{5} =$ _____

3 $\frac{13}{6} \times \frac{4}{2} =$ _____

Solve the following problems.

1 A bandage measures $2\frac{1}{4}$ inches long. The bandage is cut into a piece that is $\frac{2}{3}$ as long. In lowest terms, what is the length of the piece of bandage? Show your work.

> Convert the mixed number to an improper fraction before multiplying.

Answer _____ inch(es)

2 The dimensions of a postage stamp are $\frac{3}{4}$ inch by $\frac{7}{8}$ inch. What is the area of the stamp? Show your work.

> Area = length × width

Answer _____ square inch(es)

3 Collette had 3 partially full one-liter water bottles in the refrigerator. Each bottle contained about $\frac{2}{5}$ liter less water than it can hold. She poured $\frac{1}{2}$ of the water in each bottle into a larger bottle. How many liters of water did Collette pour into the larger bottle? Show your work.

> First, subtract to find the amount in each bottle.

Answer _____ liter(s)

Solve the following problems.

1 Harry has $1\frac{1}{2}$ kilograms of whole-wheat flour. He uses $\frac{3}{4}$ of the flour to bake bread. How much flour did he use? Explain how you found your answer.

_____

_____

_____

2 Use the diagram to shade the region with a length of $\frac{5}{12}$ unit and a width of $\frac{3}{7}$ unit.

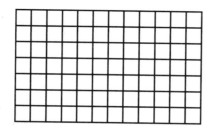

Part A What is the area of the section?

Answer _____ square unit

Part B If the length were changed to $\frac{5}{6}$ its current size, what would be the area of the shaded section?

Answer _____ square unit

3 What is the product of $1\frac{1}{7}$ and $1\frac{2}{5}$? Show your work.

Answer _____

4 Saroya needs to cover the floor of a small closet with carpet tiles. Each carpet tile measures 9 inches by 10 inches.

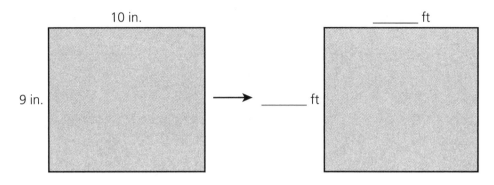

Part A What is each dimension as a fraction of a foot? Label the drawing above. Then find the area of each tile in square feet. Explain how you found your answers.

_____

_____

_____

_____

Part B The area of the closet floor is 18 square feet. If Saroya buys 32 tiles, will she have enough to cover the floor? Explain your answer.

_____

_____

_____

5 Rodney determined that the product of $\frac{11}{12}$ and $\frac{8}{12}$ is $\frac{88}{12}$.

Part A What mistake did Rodney make in his calculations?

_____

_____

Part B What is the correct product, written in lowest terms? Show your work.

Answer _____

CCSS: 5.NF.5.a, b

Multiplication and Scale

Introduction

When you multiply fractions by a whole number or another fraction, you **scale**, or resize, the number.

Use a model to help you understand scaling.

$\frac{4}{5} \times 6$ means to increase the size of $\frac{4}{5}$ by 6 times. The new value is 6 times greater.

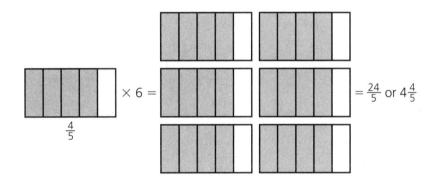

The fraction was increased from $\frac{4}{5}$ to $\frac{24}{5}$, or $4\frac{4}{5}$.

> General rules for scaling numbers:
>
> If $\frac{b}{c} < 1$, then $(a \times \frac{b}{c}) < a$.
>
> If $\frac{b}{c} = 1$, then $(a \times \frac{b}{c}) = a$.
>
> If $\frac{b}{c} > 1$, then $(a \times \frac{b}{c}) > a$.

You can also use the value of the fractions to predict the size of the product.

The product of a number and a fraction less than 1 is less than the number.

$$\frac{4}{5} \times 6 < 6 \text{ because } \frac{4}{5} \text{ is less than 1.}$$

The product of a number and a fraction greater than 1 is greater than the number.

$$\frac{5}{2} \times 3 > 3 \text{ because } \frac{5}{2} \text{ is greater than 1.}$$

$$\frac{5}{2} \times 3 = \frac{15}{2} \rightarrow \frac{15}{2} = 7\frac{1}{2}$$

> The product of a fraction and a number greater than 1 is also greater than the fraction.
>
> $$\frac{5}{2} \times 3 > \frac{5}{2}$$
>
> $$\frac{4}{5} \times 6 > \frac{4}{5}$$

Think About It

Why would the product of a number multiplied by a fraction less than 1 be less than the number?

_____

_____

2 Focused Instruction

Diagrams can help you visualize scaling. Look at the fraction first. Decide if it is greater than 1, less than 1, or equal to 1.

➤ Maggie needs to have 8 paintings for an art show. She has completed $\frac{5}{6}$ of the paintings.

Write an expression you can use to find the total number of paintings

Maggie has completed. _____

Is $\frac{5}{6}$ greater or less than 1? _____

Is the number of paintings completed greater or less than the number

of paintings she needs? _____

Use the space below to justify your answer by drawing a diagram.

> Use multiplication to find the fraction of a whole number.

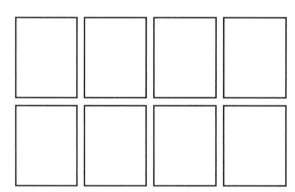

In this situation, does multiplying increase or decrease the size of the fraction?

_____

Has Maggie finished more than or less than the 8 paintings she would like to

complete? _____

➤ Franco sanded the top of a small table. The tabletop has a length of $\frac{11}{4}$ feet and a width of 3 feet. Is the area of the table greater than or less than 3 square feet?

Is the fraction $\frac{11}{4}$ greater than or less than 1? _____

Is the area greater than or less than 3? _____

Is the area greater than or less than $\frac{11}{14}$? _____

Area = *length × width*

Explain how you know.

_____

_____

Use what you know about multiplication and scaling to write > or < in the box in order to make each statement true.

1 $\frac{8}{10} \times 7$ ☐ 7

   $\frac{8}{10} \times 7$ ☐ $\frac{8}{10}$

2 $\frac{6}{3} \times 4$ ☐ 4

   $\frac{6}{3} \times 4$ ☐ $\frac{6}{3}$

3 $\frac{1}{5} \times \frac{2}{3}$ ☐ $\frac{2}{3}$

   $\frac{1}{5} \times \frac{2}{3}$ ☐ $\frac{1}{5}$

Solve the following problems.

1 Dan made a 4-foot-high scale model of a skyscraper. To get the dimensions for the model, did Dan multiply the skyscraper dimensions by a fraction less than 1 or by a fraction greater than 1?

> The model has smaller dimensions.

Answer _____

Explain your answer.

_____

_____

_____

_____

2 Mrs. Morales charges $40 per hour for tutoring. For students that need tutoring more than 3 hours per week, she charges $\frac{7}{8}$ her normal hourly rate. Does she charge more or less than her regular rate for students that are tutored more than 3 hours per week?

> Compare the fraction to 1.

Answer _____

3 A car uses 1 gallon of gas for every 17 miles traveled. A hybrid version of the same car gets $\frac{5}{3}$ of the miles as the non-hybrid car per gallon. Can the hybrid car travel more or fewer miles per gallon than the non-hybrid car?

> Remember the meaning of improper fractions.

Answer _____

Solve the following problems.

1 Write the correct symbol ($<$, $>$, or $=$) in the box to make each comparison true.

$108 \times \frac{4}{7}$ ☐ $108 \times \frac{8}{7}$

$\frac{21}{12} \times \frac{5}{4}$ ☐ $\frac{21}{12} \times \frac{3}{4}$

$2\frac{1}{6} \times \frac{3}{3}$ ☐ $\frac{4}{4} \times 2\frac{1}{6}$

2 A recipe calls for $5\frac{1}{4}$ cups of chicken broth to make 4 servings of soup. Neela wants to make 6 servings of soup. Does she need to use the amount of broth the recipe calls for, less broth, or more broth?

Answer _____

3 Look at the multiplication problem.

$$86 \times \frac{9}{12}$$

Mark True or False for each of the following statements about the multiplication problem.

	True	False
The product is greater than 86.	☐	☐
The product is less than $86 \times \frac{14}{12}$.	☐	☐
The product is less than $\frac{9}{12}$.	☐	☐

4 Michaela drives to and from work 5 days a week, from Monday through Friday. She uses $1\frac{1}{4}$ gallons of gasoline to drive to and from work every weekday.

Part A Will Michaela use more than or less than 5 gallons of gas each week driving to and from work? Explain your answer without solving the problem.

_____

_____

_____

Part B Prove your answer to Part A by finding the number of gallons Michaela will use traveling to and from work in a week. Show your work.

Answer _____ gallons

5 Which of the following comparisons are true? Select the **two** correct answers.

A $\frac{1}{4} \times 15 > 15$

B $\frac{7}{9} \times 12 > 12$

C $\frac{1}{10} \times 8 > \frac{1}{10}$

D $\frac{6}{4} \times 1\frac{1}{2} < 1\frac{1}{2}$

E $\frac{12}{7} \times \frac{1}{2} < \frac{12}{7}$

F $3\frac{5}{8} \times \frac{9}{2} < 3\frac{5}{8}$

6 Write a fraction in the boxes to make the inequality true.

$$\frac{15}{4} \times \frac{\Box}{\Box} < \frac{15}{4}$$

① Introduction

When you know how to multiply fractions and mixed numbers, you can use them to solve real-world problems.

Mimi has juice boxes that contain $\frac{1}{2}$ pint of juice each. After drinking part of a box, she has $7\frac{1}{4}$ boxes of juice remaining. How many pints of juice are remaining?

First, change $7\frac{1}{4}$ to an improper fraction. Then multiply.

$$\frac{29}{4} \times \frac{1}{2} = \frac{29}{8}$$

Convert the improper fraction to a mixed number.

$$\frac{29}{8} = 3\frac{5}{8}$$

There are $3\frac{5}{8}$ pints of juice remaining.

> To change a mixed number to an improper fraction, multiply the denominator and the whole number. Then add the numerator to the product and write the sum over the denominator.
>
> $7\frac{1}{4} = 4 \times 7 + 1 =$
> $28 + 1 = \frac{29}{4}$

Remember that you can cross out common factors to help you multiply.

A garden store claims that a tomato plant will produce about $\frac{9}{10}$ kilogram of tomatoes. The plant actually produces $\frac{4}{7}$ of the amount of tomatoes that it was claimed to produce. How many kilograms of tomatoes did the tomato plant produce?

Multiply, canceling common factors: $\dfrac{\overset{2}{\cancel{4}}}{7} \times \dfrac{9}{\underset{5}{\cancel{10}}} = \dfrac{18}{35}$

The plant produced $\frac{18}{35}$ kilogram of tomatoes.

Think About It

How do you know when multiplication is the operation needed to solve a word problem?

_____

_____

To multiply fractions, always multiply the numerators and then multiply the denominators. Put the product in lowest terms. If there is a mixed number, be sure to change it to an improper fraction before multiplying.

➤ A furniture maker uses $2\frac{1}{6}$ feet of wooden trim when building a table. An order of wooden trim contains enough trim for $1\frac{2}{3}$ tables. What is the total length of the trim, in feet, per order?

Write an expression that can be used to find the length of trim per order.

_____

What must be done to the mixed numbers before multiplying?

_____

Fill in the blanks to change each mixed number to an improper fraction.

$2\frac{1}{6} \rightarrow$ _____ $\times$ _____ $+$ _____ $=$ _____ $+$ _____ $\rightarrow \dfrac{\square}{\square}$

> The denominator of the improper fraction stays the same.

$1\frac{2}{3} \rightarrow$ _____ $\times$ _____ $+$ _____ $=$ _____ $+$ _____ $\rightarrow \dfrac{\square}{\square}$

Write a new expression that can be used to find the length of trim per order.

_____

What is the product of the numerators? _____

What is the product of the denominators? _____

What is the product as an improper fraction? _____

Fill in the blanks to change the improper fraction to a mixed number.

$\frac{65}{18} \rightarrow$ _____ $\div$ _____ $=$ _____ R _____ $\rightarrow \square \dfrac{\square}{\square}$

> To change an improper fraction to a mixed number, divide the numerator by the denominator.

What is the length of trim per order? _____

➤ Crowley rode his bicycle around a bike path that forms a loop. The bike path is $\frac{7}{8}$ mile long. He rode his bicycle 4 times around the loop and then another $\frac{1}{3}$ loop before stopping for a break. How far did Crowley ride before taking a break?

What mixed number describes the number of times Crowley rode around the loop? _____

> Each time around the loop is 1.

What two values from the problem should be multiplied?

_____

What is the improper fraction form of the number of times Crowley rode around the bike path? _____

Write an expression that can be used to find the total distance Crowley rode his bike. _____

Find the product of the numerators. _____ Of the denominators.

_____

How many miles did Crowley ride his bike? _____

What is the number of miles Crowley rode, written as a mixed number?

_____

Use what you know about multiplying fractions to answer these questions.

1   The length of a table leg is $\frac{5}{6}$ meter. If the table leg is shortened to $\frac{12}{15}$ of its current length, what is the length of the shortened table leg?

_____

2   Kimetha's brother is $1\frac{2}{3}$ yards tall. He was $\frac{4}{5}$ of that height 6 months ago. How tall was Kimetha's brother 6 months ago?

_____

Solve the following problems.

1 An inch is $\frac{1}{12}$ of a foot. A foot is $\frac{1}{3}$ of a yard. If a handle on a cooking pot is 8 inches long, how many yards long is the cooking pot handle, written in lowest terms? Show your work.

> What fraction of a yard is 1 inch?

Answer _____ yard(s)

2 The average person sleeps $\frac{1}{3}$ of each day. Assuming there are 365 days in a year, for about how many whole days does the average person sleep in a year? Show your work.

> Round the product to the nearest whole number.

Answer _____ days

3 To change a village parking law, 60 votes are required. If $\frac{9}{20}$ of the 100 people in a village vote to change the law, are there enough votes to change the law? Explain. If not, tell how many more votes are needed.

> Write the product as a whole number, by dividing.

_____

_____

Solve the following problems.

1 Rebecca is following the recipe to make biscuits.

> **Biscuits**
>
> 2 c flour
>
> 1 tsp sugar
>
> 1 tbsp baking powder
>
> 1 tsp salt
>
> 8 tbsp butter
>
> $\frac{3}{4}$ c milk

The recipe makes 24 biscuits. If Rebecca needs $\frac{1}{4}$ that many biscuits, how much milk should she use?

Answer _____ cup

2 Mr. Falkner has written a company report every 3 months for the last 6 years. If $\frac{2}{3}$ of the reports show his company earns more money than it spends, how many reports show his company spending more money than it earns? Show your work.

Answer _____ reports

3 Rami is making a chain of paper stars. Each star measures $4\frac{2}{6}$ inches across.

$4\frac{2}{6}$ in.

The chain must have 11 stars to reach from one side of a window to the other. Which expression can be used to find the length of the chain from the center of the window to the side of the window? Select the **two** correct answers.

A $11 \times 4\frac{2}{6}$

B $5\frac{1}{2} \times 4\frac{1}{3}$

C $11 \times \frac{28}{6}$

D $\frac{11}{2} \times \frac{13}{3}$

E $11 \times \frac{24}{6}$

F $\frac{11}{2} \times \frac{12}{3}$

4 Andre uses $\frac{7}{12}$ kilogram of bronze to cast a small sculpture. He receives an order for 15 of these sculptures.

   Part A   How much bronze does Andre need to make the sculptures? Show your work.

   Answer _____ kilogram(s)

   Part B   Andre makes another sculpture that uses $2\frac{2}{5}$ times as much bronze as the small sculpture. How many kilograms of bronze does this sculpture need? Show your work.

   Answer _____ kilogram(s)

5 Selma is building a birdhouse. She uses a piece of wood that measures $\frac{3}{4}$ foot by $\frac{5}{6}$ foot for the base of the house. What is the area of the birdhouse's base?

   A $\frac{4}{5}$ square foot

   B $\frac{5}{8}$ square foot

   C   1 square foot

   D $\frac{9}{10}$ square foot

Introduction

Dividing by a fraction means to divide or separate into smaller portions. The quotient describes how many of those portions there are.

This diagram shows $2 \div \frac{1}{3}$.

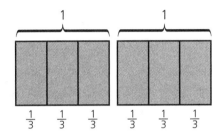

There are 2 whole units divided into portions of $\frac{1}{3}$. The total number of $\frac{1}{3}$ portions is 6.

To divide by a fraction, multiply by the **reciprocal** of the divisor. A reciprocal is the inverse of a fraction, such as $\frac{1}{3}$ and $\frac{3}{1}$.

$$2 \div \frac{1}{3} = 2 \times \frac{3}{1} = \frac{6}{1}$$

Any number divided by 1 is itself, so $2 \times \frac{3}{1} = 6$ or $2 \div \frac{1}{3} = 6$.

> The product of a fraction and its reciprocal is 1.
> $$\frac{1}{3} \times \frac{3}{1} = \frac{3}{3}$$
> $$\frac{3}{3} = 1$$

To divide a fraction by a whole number, first rewrite the whole number as a fraction with a denominator of 1. Then multiply by the reciprocal.

Josef has $\frac{1}{7}$ of a batch of pudding left after dinner. He separates the remaining pudding evenly into 4 bowls. What fraction of the batch of pudding is in each bowl?

Divide: $\frac{1}{7} \div 4$

> Use the reciprocal of the divisor, which may or may not be a fraction in the original problem.

Rewrite the problem as a multiplication problem using the reciprocal of the divisor: $\frac{1}{7} \times \frac{1}{4}$, because 4 written in fraction form is $\frac{4}{1}$.

Multiply: $\frac{1}{7} \times \frac{1}{4} = \frac{1}{28}$.

Each cup contains $\frac{1}{28}$ of the batch of pudding.

Think About It

Why do you think it is possible to multiply by a reciprocal and still find the same answer as when dividing?

_____

_____

2 Focused Instruction

Diagrams can help you understand dividing with fractions. They can help you visualize what type of number you will have for an answer.

➤ Olga's cellphone used $\frac{1}{10}$ of its battery power when it was unplugged for 2 hours. What fraction of its total battery power did the cellphone use per hour?

What is being divided in the problem, the amount of battery power or the

number of hours? _____

Write a division expression that can be used to find the amount of battery power

used per hour. _____

Draw a picture that can be used to model the expression.

> Create a fraction model that shows tenths.

What is the reciprocal of 2? _____

> How do you write a whole number as a fraction?

Write a multiplication expression that can be used to find the amount of battery power used per hour. _____

What fraction of the battery power did Olga's phone use per hour? _____

➤ What is $6 \div \frac{1}{3}$?

Draw a picture that can be used to model the expression.

> How many wholes should you draw? Into how many sections should you divide each whole?

Based on your model, how many $\frac{1}{3}$'s are in 6? _____

What is the reciprocal of $\frac{1}{3}$? _____

Use multiplication to prove that your model shows the quotient.

_____

Was your model accurate? _____

Which method is faster when dividing by a fraction or dividing a fraction by a number: drawing a picture or multiplying by the reciprocal?

_____

Use what you know about dividing with fractions to find these quotients.

1 $\frac{1}{9} \div 8 = $ _____

2 $14 \div \frac{1}{5} = $ _____

3 $25 \div \frac{1}{6} = $ _____

Solve the following problems.

1 Write and solve a division expression you could use to find how many nickels are in $7. Show your work.

> What fraction of a dollar is a nickel?

Answer _____ nickels

2 Divide $\frac{1}{4}$ by 3. Show your work.

> For which number do you need to find the reciprocal?

Answer _____

3 A cheese cracker factory used $\frac{1}{16}$ ton of flour to make enough crackers for 100 boxes of crackers. How many tons of flour did each box of crackers contain?

> To divide, write the whole number as a fraction with a denominator of 1.

Answer _____ ton

Explain how you found your answer.

_____

_____

_____

Solve the following problems.

1 Irma bought 2 pounds of potatoes to make breakfast tacos. She put $\frac{1}{12}$ pound of potatoes in each taco. If she used all the potatoes, how many breakfast tacos did Irma make? Show your work.

Answer _____ breakfast tacos

2 Bruce needs $\frac{2}{3}$ of a ball of yarn to knit a potholder. He has 14 balls of yarn. Which expressions can be used to find the number of potholders he can knit? Select the **two** correct answers.

A $14 \div \frac{2}{3}$

B $\frac{1}{14} \times \frac{2}{3}$

C $14 \times \frac{3}{2}$

D $\frac{2}{3} \times \frac{14}{1}$

E $\frac{2}{3} \div 14$

F $\frac{2}{3} \times \frac{1}{14}$

3 A cook cut a piece of sausage measuring $\frac{1}{6}$ yard long into 5 equal pieces.

Part A What is the length of each piece of sausage?

Answer _____ yard

Part B Explain how you found your answer.

_____

_____

_____

4 Hal is planting beans in a row that is 20 meters long. He plants a bean seed every $\frac{1}{4}$ meter.

Part A How many bean seeds can Hal plant in this row? Explain your answer.

_____

_____

_____

Part B Would Hal be able to plant more seeds or fewer seeds if he planted a bean seed every $\frac{1}{5}$ meter? How many seeds can he plant if he plants them $\frac{1}{5}$ meter apart?

_____

_____

_____

_____

5 Write the corresponding multiplication expression that can be used to find the quotient of each division expression and the quotient.

	Multiplication Expression	Quotient
$\frac{1}{7} \div 13$		
$20 \div \frac{1}{10}$		
$\frac{1}{5} \div 64$		
$11 \div \frac{1}{8}$		

Introduction

You can use what you know about dividing with fractions to solve real-world problems. Think about what is being separated or divided. This will help you put the numbers used as the dividend and divisor in the correct order.

Sometimes you will divide a fraction by a whole number.

A bag of trail mix weighed $\frac{1}{2}$ pound. The trail mix was shared evenly by 5 friends. How much trail mix did each friend eat?

The trail mix was separated into 5 equal groups, so divide the weight of the trail mix by 5: $\frac{1}{2} \div 5$.

Multiply by the reciprocal of the divisor, 5, to find the total weight of trail mix each friend ate.

$$\frac{1}{2} \times \frac{1}{5} = \frac{1 \times 1}{2 \times 5} = \frac{1}{10}$$

> The reciprocal is the number that multiplies another number for a product of 1.

Each friend ate $\frac{1}{10}$ pound of trail mix.

Sometimes you will divide a whole number by a fraction.

Laila bought 18 yards of ribbon and cut it into pieces that were $\frac{1}{3}$ yard long. How many pieces of ribbon did Laila have?

The 18 yards of ribbon were separated into smaller pieces measuring $\frac{1}{3}$ yard, so divide: $18 \div \frac{1}{3}$.

Multiply by the reciprocal of the divisor, $\frac{1}{3}$, to find the number of pieces of ribbon.

$$18 \times \frac{3}{1} = \frac{18 \times 3}{1} = \frac{54}{1}$$

> A number divided by 1 is that number.

There were 54 total pieces of ribbon.

Think About It

Why is it important to have the numbers in the dividend and divisor in the correct place, unlike in multiplication?

_____

_____

② Focused Instruction

Always read word problems carefully. Think about what you already know and use that to help you find the solution.

➤ Jackie has $40 in quarters. How many quarters does Jackie have?

Is the $40 separated into quarters, or are the quarters separated into smaller units?

_____

Which number is the dividend? _____

What is the fraction value of a quarter, in lowest terms? _____

Which number is the divisor? _____

Write a division expression that can be used to find the number of quarters

Jackie has. _____

What is the reciprocal of the divisor? _____

Write a multiplication expression that can be used to find the number

of quarters Jackie has. _____

What is the product of the whole number and the numerator of the

fraction? _____

What is the denominator? _____

How many quarters does Jackie have? _____

> To find the reciprocal, switch the numerator and the denominator.

> A number divided by 1 is the number.

➤ Micah is training his dog for a competition. He sets up cones along a sidewalk that is $\frac{1}{8}$ mile long. There are 12 cones that are evenly spaced along the sidewalk. How far apart are the cones from one another?

Is the sidewalk divided into smaller sections or are the cones separated into groups?

_____

What is the dividend of the problem? _____

What is the divisor of the problem? _____

Write a division expression that can be used to find how far apart the

cones are from one another. _____

What is the reciprocal of the divisor? _____

Write a multiplication expression that can be used to find how far

apart the cones are from one another. _____

What is the product of the numerators? _____

What is the product of the denominators? _____

How far apart are the cones from one another? _____

> Write a whole number as a fraction by giving it a denominator of 1.

Use what you know about dividing with fractions to answer these questions.

1 Mrs. Kaplan's class painted $\frac{1}{5}$ of a school mural. There are
   17 students in her class. How much of the mural did each student in her
   class paint on average?

   _____

2 Lin had 30 books. How many days did it take her to read them if each day
   she read $\frac{1}{10}$ of a book?

   _____

Solve the following problems.

1 A report is 35 pages long. There is a diagram every $\frac{1}{4}$ page.

> The pages are divided into sections of $\frac{1}{4}$ page each.

> **Part A** Write an expression that can be used to find the number of diagrams used in the report.

> Answer _____

> **Part B** What is the total number of diagrams used in the report?

> Answer _____ diagrams

2 A large rainwater barrel contains 50 gallons of water. Each plant in a garden is given $\frac{1}{8}$ gallon of water. How many plants can be watered if the rain barrel is full? Show your work.

> Divide the total amount of water into parts of $\frac{1}{8}$ gallon.

Answer _____ plants

3 Kaijo was preparing for a party. He made $\frac{1}{7}$ pound of seasoning to use on the grilled chicken. He seasoned 16 chicken legs with an equal amount of seasoning. How much seasoning did Kaijo use on each chicken leg?

> Is the seasoning being divided or are the chicken legs being divided?

Answer _____ pound

Solve the following problems.

1   Mr. Miner's art classes did yarn art. Each student began with a piece of yarn.
Mr. Miner had a spool of yarn with $\frac{1}{20}$ mile of yarn. He gave each of his
66 students an equal length of yarn.

   Part A What is the length of yarn that each student received? Show your
   work.

   Answer _____ mile

   Part B One student cut her piece of yarn into 3 pieces of equal length.
   What was the length of each piece of yarn? Explain how you found
   your answer.

   _____

   _____

   _____

2 Lenore is performing a violin solo at a concert in a week. She set a goal to practice her song for at least 15 hours before her performance. The song she will play is $\frac{1}{5}$ hour long. Which equations show how many times Lenore will play the song in her 15 hours of practice time? Select the **two** correct answers.

A $\quad \frac{1}{5} + 15 = \frac{1}{75}$

B $\quad \frac{1}{5} \times \frac{15}{1} = \frac{15}{5}$

C $\quad 15 \div \frac{1}{5} = 75$

D $\quad 15 \times \frac{5}{1} = 75$

E $\quad \frac{1}{5} \times \frac{1}{15} = \frac{1}{75}$

F $\quad 15 \times \frac{5}{1} = \frac{75}{15}$

3 Complete the equation that describes each situation.

Situation	Equation
3 feet of fabric cut into $\frac{1}{6}$ foot strips	$3 \div \frac{1}{6} = 3 \times \dfrac{\Box}{\Box}$
10 lasagnas served in pieces that are $\frac{1}{9}$ of a pan	$\Box \div \dfrac{\Box}{\Box} = \Box \times \Box$
$\frac{1}{11}$ of a packet of construction paper split among 22 students	$\frac{1}{11} \div \Box = \dfrac{\Box}{\Box} \times \dfrac{\Box}{\Box}$

4 A banana bread recipe calls for the ingredients shown for 1 small loaf.

> ### Banana Bread
>
> $\frac{1}{4}$ c butter $\frac{3}{4}$ c flour
>
> $\frac{1}{2}$ c sugar $\frac{1}{4}$ tsp baking soda
>
> 1 egg $\frac{1}{8}$ tsp salt
>
> 2 bananas $\frac{1}{4}$ tsp vanilla

Part A If the recipe were split into 4 mini loaf pans, how much butter and sugar would be used in each pan? Show your work.

Butter _____ cup

Sugar _____ cup

Part B Would there be more baking soda or salt in each pan? Explain how you know.

_____

_____

_____

_____

Number and Operations— Fractions

Solve the following problems.

1 A song is $2\frac{3}{4}$ minutes long. The radio station pays the record company a fee every time the song is played.

   Part A If the song is played 15 times in a week, how many minutes did the song play during that week? Show your work.

   Answer _____ minutes

   Part B If the radio station paid the record company $2 per minute to play the song during the week, how much did the radio station pay the record company? Explain how you found your answer.

   _____

   _____

   _____

2 Which of the following comparisons are true? Select the **two** correct answers.

A $(8 \times 2\frac{5}{6}) < 8$

B $(10 \times \frac{6}{7}) < \frac{6}{7}$

C $(5 \times 1\frac{1}{3}) < 1\frac{1}{3}$

D $(2 \times 1\frac{2}{5}) > 2$

E $(6 \times \frac{8}{2}) > 6$

F $(7 \times \frac{3}{7}) > 7$

3 Caroline ate $\frac{3}{8}$ of half of a bag of popcorn. What part of the whole bag of popcorn did Caroline eat?

A 16

B $\frac{3}{4}$

C $\frac{7}{8}$

D $\frac{3}{16}$

4 Rena put cereal in a bowl so the bowl was $\frac{3}{7}$ full. Rena added milk to the bowl so that it was $\frac{6}{8}$ full. How much of the bowl was filled with just milk? Show your work.

Answer _____ bowl

5 A pretzel shop uses $\frac{8}{10}$ pound of butter in a batch of original pretzel dough. A new pretzel flavor is being tested. A test batch is made with $\frac{14}{20}$ pound of butter less than the original pretzels.

Part A How much butter is used to make the test batch of pretzels? Show your work.

Answer _____ pound

Part B The test batch dough is evenly separated into 3 small bowls. How much butter is in the dough in each bowl? Explain how you found your answer.

_____

_____

_____

6 Mark True or False for each equation.

	True	False
$\frac{6}{5} + \frac{1}{4} = \frac{7}{9}$	☐	☐
$\frac{1}{7} \div 10 = \frac{1}{70}$	☐	☐
$\frac{3}{4} - \frac{1}{2} = \frac{1}{4}$	☐	☐
$\frac{8}{10} \times \frac{2}{3} = \frac{8}{15}$	☐	☐
$16 \div \frac{1}{12} = \frac{1}{192}$	☐	☐

7 Twelve people will share 3 pounds of watermelon. If they share equally, what fraction of a pound will each person get? Write your answer in lowest terms.

Answer _____ pound

8 A tablet screen measures $10\frac{1}{2}$ inches by $7\frac{1}{8}$ inches. What is the area of the tablet screen?

Answer _____ square inches

9 What is the quotient of $\frac{1}{6} \div 20$?

Answer _____

10 An artist uses driftwood to make ornaments. A piece of driftwood measures 6 feet long. The artist cuts the driftwood into pieces that are $\frac{1}{2}$ foot long. Into how many pieces can he cut the driftwood? Show your work.

Answer _____ pieces

11 Angela wants to retile the backsplash in her kitchen using 4-inch-by-4-inch tiles, as shown here.

4 in.

4 in.

Part A What is the area of each tile in square feet? Explain how you got your answer.

_____

_____

_____

Part B If the area of the backsplash is 24 square feet, how many tiles does Angela need to cover the entire backsplash? Show your work.

Answer _____ tiles

Measurement and Data

In grade 4, you learned about customary and metric units, using line plots, and solving for the area and perimeter of rectangles. Now you can use what you know about measurement to convert units, compare data on line plots, and find the volume of regular and irregular figures.

LESSON 27 Measurement Conversions In this lesson, you will convert measurements within the customary system and the metric system.

LESSON 28 Measurement Data on Line Plots In this lesson, you will make line plots to show data sets and you will use line plots to draw conclusions about the data.

LESSON 29 Understanding Volume In this lesson, you will stack unit cubes and draw models to find the volume.

LESSON 30 Volume of Rectangular Prisms In this lesson, you will use unit cubes and the volume formula to find the volume of rectangular prisms.

LESSON 31 Volume of Irregular Figures In this lesson, you will find the volume of an irregular figure by separating figures to find the sum of multiple volumes.

Measurement Conversions

CCSS: 5.MD.1

1 Introduction

In the United States, you typically measure using the **customary system.** In many other parts of the world, people use the **metric system.** The table shows units that can be used to measure length, capacity, and mass or weight in each system.

MEASUREMENT EQUIVALENCE

	Length	Capacity	Weight/Mass	Time
Customary System	1 ft = 12 in. 1 yd = 3 ft 1 mi = 5,280 ft 1 mi = 1,760 yd	1 pt = 2 c 1 qt = 2 pt 1 gal = 4 qt	1 lb = 16 oz 1 T = 2,000 lb	1 min = 60 sec 1 hr = 60 min 1 day = 24 hr
Metric System	1 cm = 10 mm 1 m = 100 cm 1 km = 1,000 m	1 L = 1,000 mL	1 kg = 1,000 g	

You can convert from one unit of measurement to another within the same system. For example, you can convert from inches to feet to yards because they are all units of length. In the same way, you can convert from milliliters to liters because they are both units of capacity.

To convert a larger unit to a smaller unit, multiply. To convert a smaller unit to a larger unit, divide. The number you multiply or divide by is called a **conversion factor.**

> When you convert a larger unit to a smaller unit, you end up with more units.
>
> When you convert a smaller unit to a larger unit, you end up with fewer units.

Bartok ordered a new refrigerator. The refrigerator space in his kitchen measures 4 feet wide. The refrigerator he ordered has a width of 36 inches. How much space will remain after installing the refrigerator?

To solve this problem, first find the relationship between inches and feet: 1 ft = 12 in. Feet are larger than inches, so multiply to find the width of the space in inches.

$$4 \text{ ft} \times 12 \text{ in.} = 48 \text{ in.}$$

To find the amount of space left after installing the new refrigerator, subtract the width of the refrigerator from the width of the space: 48 in. − 36 in. = 12 in.

Think About It

Describe an example of an everyday measurement you might make or get in different units.

_____

_____

_____

 Focused Instruction

In the metric system, units are expressed as multiples of 10 of the base unit. This means you can convert metric units by multiplying or dividing by a power of 10. You can do that by moving the decimal point left or right.

➤ Coach Barnes had 25 liters of water for her cheer team to drink during a competition. At the end of the day, she found that her team drank all but 250 milliliters of water. How many liters did the team drink during the competition?

How many milliliters are in 1 liter? _____

Will you multiply or divide to change liters to milliliters?

_____

Write an expression to show how you will change the original number of liters to

milliliters in this problem. _____

Which factor is a multiple of 10? _____

How can you write this factor as 10 raised to a power? _____

Will the number of milliliters be greater than or less than 25?

_____

Which direction should you move the decimal point to multiply by a power

of 10? _____ To divide? _____

How will you move the decimal point to find the number of milliliters the team started with?

_____

> You worked with powers of 10 in Lesson 6.

> Are milliliters larger than or smaller than liters?

How many milliliters of water did the team have to start? _____

How can you find the number of milliliters of water the team drank?

_____

How many milliliters of water did the team drink? _____

How can you change the number of milliliters of water the team drank back to liters?

_____

How many liters of water did the team drink? _____

Sometimes you may need to use more than one step to convert measurements. Work with a partner to answer these questions.

➤ Using a measuring tape, measure your partner's height in inches. How tall is your partner in inches, in feet, and in yards?

What is your partner's height in inches? _____

Is a foot larger or smaller than an inch? _____

To convert inches to feet, what operation should you use?

_____

How many inches are in 1 foot? _____

How can you convert your partner's height to feet?

_____

What is your partner's height in feet? _____

Is a yard longer or shorter than an inch? _____

Is a yard longer or shorter than a foot? _____

To convert inches to yards or feet to yards, what operation should you use?

_____

> It may be necessary to write the height in the form of a mixed number.

Describe two methods you can use to convert your partner's height from inches to yards.

> What units are between the unit you start with and the unit you want to end with?

_____

_____

What is your partner's height in yards? _____

Use what you know about converting measurements to solve these conversions.

1 15 liters = _____ milliliters

2 167 ounces = _____ pounds

3 28 kilometers = _____ centimeters

4 36 cups = _____ gallons

Solve the following problems.

1   A rosebush stands 4 feet tall. A lilac bush stands 60 inches tall. Which bush is taller? Show your work.

Convert one of the heights so both have the same units.

Answer _____

2   A newborn hippopotamus can weigh between 20 and 50 kilograms. What is a newborn hippopotamus's weight range, in grams? Show your work.

Convert the upper and lower values in the range to find the new range.

Answer between _____ grams and _____ grams

3   Martina and Pablo's parents are replacing their water heater. The old water heater only held enough water for 2 people. They are replacing it with a water heater that has a capacity for 4 people. The old water heater could hold 50 quarts of water per person. The new water heater will hold 15 gallons per person. How many more gallons will the new water heater hold than the old water heater? Explain how you found your answer.

Find the capacity of each water heater and then convert to gallons.

_____

_____

_____

_____

Solve the following problems.

1 Which expressions can be used to find the number of seconds in 2 days? Select the **two** correct answers.

A 48×60

B $3{,}600 \times 24$

C $2 \times 24 \times 60$

D $48 \times 60 \times 60$

E $24 \times 60 \times 60$

F $2 \times (24 \times 3{,}600)$

2 A pluot is a fruit bred from a mix of a plum and an apricot. An average pluot tree has a mature height of 9 feet. An aprium is also a type of plum and apricot cross. A full-size aprium tree can grow to about 117.6 inches. Is an aprium tree taller or shorter than a pluot tree? Explain.

_____

_____

_____

3 Select an option in each set and fill in each blank to make the equations true.

78 meters [$\times$, $\div$] _____ = _____ kilometer(s)

1,254 cups [$\times$, $\div$] _____ [$\times$, $\div$] _____ =

_____ quart(s)

9 tons [$\times$, $\div$] _____ [$\times$, $\div$] _____ = 288,000 ounces

1.5 days [$\times$, $\div$] 24 [$\times$, $\div$] _____ = _____ minute(s)

4 Ned uses 120 pints of water to take a 5-minute shower, Sandy uses 100 quarts for a 10-minute shower, and Landon uses 24.8 gallons for an 8-minute shower. Who uses the most gallons of water per minute, and how many gallons did that person use? Explain.

_____

_____

_____

5 The largest swimming pool in the world is San Alfonso del Mar pool in Algarrobo, Chile. It is 1,013 meters long. How long is the pool in kilometers? Show your work.

Answer _____ kilometer(s)

6 Gabe traveled by train from Los Angeles to Chicago. The train ride was 3,645 kilometers and took approximately 42 hours. What was the speed of the train in meters per hour? Round your answer to the nearest whole number. Show your work.

Answer _____ meters per hour

7 Kyle needs 48 ounces of flour. What combination of bags of flour could he buy, and how many of them does he need? Explain.

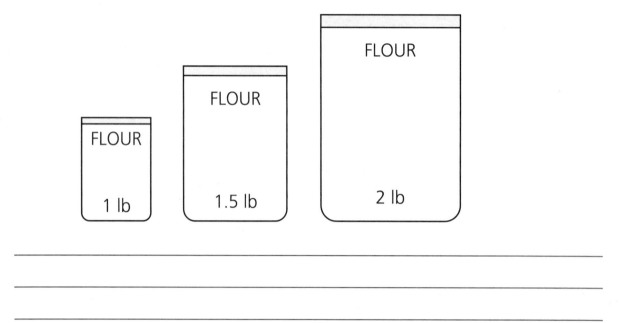

_____

_____

_____

8 The chart below lists the regulation sizes and weights of the balls used in various sports.

Type of Ball	Circumference	Weight
golf ball	1.68 in.	1.62 oz
soccer ball	2.25–2.33 ft	0.875–1 lb
baseball	9–9.25 in.	5–5.25 oz
table tennis ball	1.57 in.	0.006 lb
basketball	29.5–30 in.	1.25–1.375 lb
bowling ball	not more than 2.25 ft	not more than 16 lb
tennis ball	8.07–8.48 in.	2–2.17 oz
volleyball	25.6–26.4 in.	9.2–9.9 oz

Part A For each pair listed below, identify which ball is larger or heavier.

• **larger:** soccer ball or basketball? _____

• **heavier:** volleyball or soccer ball? _____

Part B Nestor is playing tennis with a ball that is 0.628 foot in circumference and weighs 0.125 pound. Is this a regulation tennis ball in terms of size and weight? Explain.

_____

_____

_____

_____

_____

LESSON

28 Measurement Data on Line Plots

CCSS: 5.MD.2

 Introduction

A **line plot** can be used to show and compare **data,** or information. A line plot is a diagram that displays data on a number line. Each single value is represented by an X.

A student measured the lengths of some crayons. The measurements, in centimeters, are listed. Show this data in a line plot.

$$6\frac{1}{4}, 7, 6\frac{3}{4}, 6, 6\frac{1}{2}, 6\frac{1}{4}, 7, 7\frac{1}{2}, 6\frac{3}{4}, 6\frac{1}{4}$$

The shortest length is 6 centimeters. The longest length is $7\frac{1}{2}$ centimeters. Draw a number line from at least 6 to $7\frac{1}{2}$. Use intervals of $\frac{1}{4}$. Then draw an X to represent each crayon. Give the line plot a title, telling what it shows.

CRAYON LENGTHS

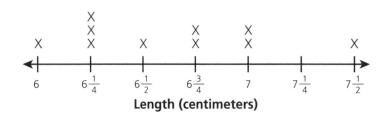

Length (centimeters)

> A line plot is sometimes called a dot plot. Then it uses dots instead of Xs.

You can use the information in line plots to analyze data and solve problems.

Look at the line plot above. What is the difference between the length of the longest crayon and the length of the shortest crayon?

Find the length farthest to the left: 6 centimeters

Find the length farthest to the right: $7\frac{1}{2}$ centimeters

Subtract to find the difference: $7\frac{1}{2} - 6 = 1\frac{1}{2}$ centimeters

> Range is the difference between the greatest value and the least value in a data set.

228 UNIT 5 Measurement and Data

© The Continental Press, Inc. DUPLICATING THIS MATERIAL IS ILLEGAL.

Think About It

What other kinds of information might you show on a line plot?

_____

_____

Read the data on a line plot and use it to answer questions about the data set. There is one X on the line plot for each piece of data in a data set.

➤ The volumes of bottles of different brands of bottled water sold at a store are shown in the line plot. If 1 bottle of each brand of water is purchased, how much water is purchased altogether?

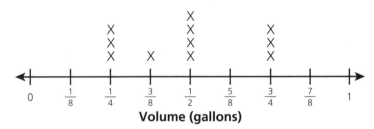

WATER BOTTLES

Volume (gallons)

What operation can you use to find the total amount of water purchased?

_____

List all the volumes of each water bottle in gallons.

_____

What must you do to add fractions?

_____

What number can you use as a common denominator for these fractions?

_____

List the volumes of the bottles with common denominators.

_____

How much water was purchased altogether? _____

> How many Xs are over $\frac{1}{4}$? Over $\frac{3}{8}$?

> To add fractions, add the numerators. The denominator stays the same.

Use information in a set of data to create a line plot. Look at the information carefully. Then organize it in a line plot.

➤ A sandwich stand offers sandwiches with different amounts of meat. Diners can choose from $\frac{1}{4}$-pound, $\frac{1}{3}$-pound, $\frac{1}{2}$-pound, or 1-pound sandwiches. Each sandwich sold is recorded on a board to track the meat used. The board shows the weight of meat in the sandwiches that were sold.

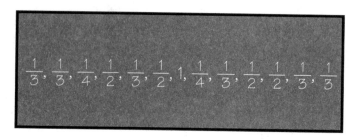

$$\frac{1}{3}, \frac{1}{3}, \frac{1}{4}, \frac{1}{2}, \frac{1}{3}, \frac{1}{2}, 1, \frac{1}{4}, \frac{1}{3}, \frac{1}{2}, \frac{1}{2}, \frac{1}{3}, \frac{1}{3}$$

What is the smallest amount of meat? _____

What is the largest amount of meat? _____

What should the range on a number line be to show this data?

_____

> It might help to put the data in order from least to greatest.

How many $\frac{1}{4}$-pound sandwiches were sold? _____ How many $\frac{1}{3}$-pound sandwiches? _____ How many $\frac{1}{2}$-pound sandwiches? _____ How many 1-pound sandwiches? _____

How many Xs do you need to show the $\frac{1}{4}$-pound sandwiches? _____

What is true about the number of Xs on the line plot and the number of sandwiches?

_____

Draw a line plot to represent the data.

> Use one X for each sandwich.

⟵——————————————————⟶

Use the line plot below to answer these questions.

PAGES READ

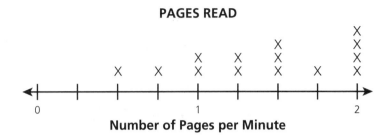

Number of Pages per Minute

1 What is the most common number of pages read per minute? _____

2 What is the least number of pages read per minute? _____

3 What is the difference between the greatest and least number of pages read

per minute? _____

Solve the following problems.

1   The line plot shows the rate at which some students walk to school.

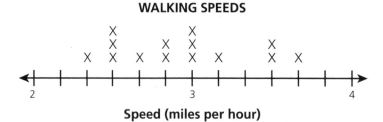

WALKING SPEEDS

Speed (miles per hour)

> Each X stands for one person.

How many students walk at a rate that is greater than $2\frac{2}{3}$ miles per hour?

Answer _____ students

2   The line plot shows the weights, in ounces, of 9 lab mice.

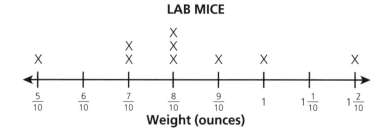

LAB MICE

Weight (ounces)

> The median weight is the weight in the middle. There will be an equal number of weights to the right and left of it.

What is the median weight of the 9 mice?

Answer _____ ounce(s)

3   A movie theater is showing movies of the lengths shown by the line plot.

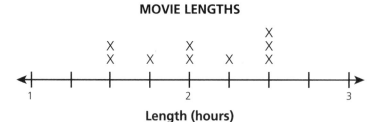

MOVIE LENGTHS

Length (hours)

> Decide what fraction each tick mark represents.

If a movie fan were to watch each movie once, how many minutes would she spend at the theater? Explain.

_____

_____

_____

Solve the following problems.

Use the line plot to answer problems 1 and 2.

RAINFALL FOR A WEEK

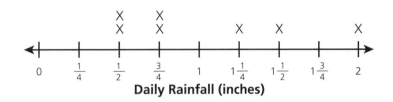

Daily Rainfall (inches)

1 What is the total amount of rain that fell during the week?

Answer _____ inches

2 Which rainfall amounts occurred on more than one day? Select the **two** correct answers.

A $\frac{1}{4}$ inch

B $\frac{1}{2}$ inch

C $\frac{3}{4}$ inch

D $1\frac{1}{4}$ inches

E $1\frac{1}{2}$ inches

F   2 inches

3   Reggie created his own recipe for bean soup. He looked at different recipes to compare the amount of beans used in each. This line plot shows the amount of beans, in cups, needed for some recipes.

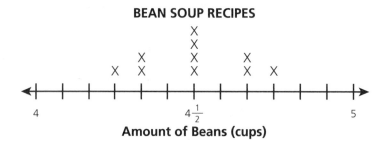

Part A What is the most common amount of beans used in the recipes?

Answer _____ cups

Part B Reggie found the average amount of beans in the three recipes that call for the greatest amount of beans. He based the amount of beans in his recipe on this amount. What is the average amount of beans used in the three recipes with the greatest amounts? Explain.

_____

_____

4   Dwayne recorded the amount of water he drank each day for a week.

> Dwayne's Log
>
> Sunday: $2\frac{1}{10}$ L   Thursday: $1\frac{4}{5}$ L
>
> Monday: $1\frac{1}{2}$ L   Friday: $2\frac{1}{10}$ L
>
> Tuesday: $1\frac{8}{10}$ L   Saturday: $1\frac{3}{5}$ L
>
> Wednesday: $2\frac{1}{10}$ L

Part A   Make a line plot to display the data.

Part B   It is recommended that a person drink $1\frac{9}{10}$ liters of water per day to stay healthy. On average, did Dwayne drink enough water per day? Explain how you found your answer.

_____

_____

_____

_____

5 Mr. Mason's classroom has been growing pea plants. After several days, the students measured the heights of the plants. The line plot below shows the heights of the pea plants.

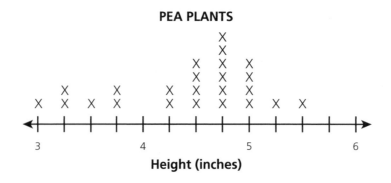

Part A How many plants did the class measure?

Answer _____ plants

Part B Select the correct option in each set to make the following statement true.

The tallest plant is [$2\frac{1}{2}$, $4\frac{3}{4}$, $5\frac{1}{2}$,   6] inches tall. The shortest plant is [$2\frac{1}{2}$,   3, $3\frac{1}{4}$, $5\frac{1}{2}$] inches tall. The difference between the shortest plant and the tallest plant is [$1\frac{3}{4}$,   2, $2\frac{1}{2}$,   3] inches.

Understanding Volume

CCSS: 5.MD.3.a, b; 4

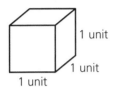 **Introduction**

Volume is a measure of the amount of space an object takes up. It can be measured by finding the number of cubic units it takes to fill the object without overlapping and without spaces between the units. A **cubic unit** is the volume of a cube that has a side length of 1 unit. This type of cube is known as a **unit cube.** It is 1 unit wide, 1 unit long, and 1 unit tall.

A cube with side lengths measuring 1 unit has a volume of 1 cubic unit, or 1 unit^3.

> A cube is a rectangular prism with sides of equal length.

A small box that is 2 inches wide, 2 inches long, and 6 inches tall arrives in the mail. What is the volume of the box in cubic inches?

To find the volume of the box, you can stack unit cubes inside the box. Think of making layers of cubes. One layer has 2 rows of 2 cubes. So there are 4 cubes in a layer. One layer is 4 cubic inches.

> The side length of the unit cube can be measured in any unit of length. A side length of 1 centimeter means the volume is 1 cubic centimeter (cm^3).

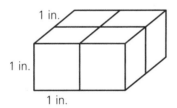

The box is 6 inches high. So it has 6 layers like the one above. There are 24 cubes in the entire box, so the volume is 24 cubic inches.

> Cubic inches can be written as cubic inches or in.^{3}

Think About It

Why might it be important to be able to measure the volume of a box used to ship a package?

_____

_____

Work with a partner to build a model using unit cubes to help you understand this volume problem.

➤ Ansel's dad ordered a new chair. The chair was delivered in a box that measured 6 feet long, 3 feet wide, and 5 feet tall. What is the volume of the box?

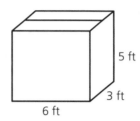

5 ft
3 ft
6 ft

Build a model of the box using unit cubes.

First, make a row of unit cubes. How many cubes will be in a row? _____

How many rows of unit cubes are in each layer? _____

How many unit cubes are in each layer? _____

How many layers of cubes are in the model? _____

Since each layer has the same number of cubes in it, what operation can you use to find the number of cubes in the total number of layers?

_____

Multiply the number of layers by the number of unit cubes in each layer.

_____

How many unit cubes are there in all? _____

What is the volume of the box? _____

> Think of the row as the length of the box.

> How high is the box?

> Each unit cube has a volume of 1 cubic foot (1 ft^3).

Count the cubes that make up a rectangular prism to find the volume. You will not be able to see all the cubes.

➤ The rectangular prism below is made up of cubes measuring 1 yard on each edge.

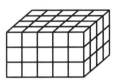

Can you see all the cubes in the figure? _____

How can you tell how many cubes are in the figure?

_____

What is the volume of each unit cube? _____

How many unit cubes are in the bottom layer of the prism? _____

How many layers are in the model? _____

Multiply the number of layers by the number of unit cubes in each layer.

_____

How many unit cubes are there in all? _____

What is the volume of the rectangular prism? _____

> How can you tell what
> cubes are hidden
> behind others?

Use what you know about volume to find the volume of these objects.

1   _____

2 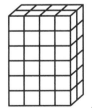 _____

Solve the following problems.

1 A closet is 5 feet wide, 4 feet long, and 7 feet tall. Explain how to find the volume of the closet using boxes that measure 1 foot on each edge.

> Think of the closet in layers. What is the volume of one layer?

_____

_____

2 A rectangular figure has one layer filled with the cubes shown.

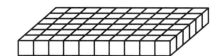

> If the figure is 4 units tall, how many layers like the model shown will the figure have?

If the figure is 4 units tall, write an expression that can be used to find the volume of the figure.

Answer _____

3 Luca is packing a truck's cargo section with boxes. Each box is 1 cubic yard. If the truck's cargo section is 2 yards wide by 2 yards high by 5 yards deep, how many boxes can fit?

> Count the number of boxes measuring 1 cubic yard that can be stacked in each layer.

Answer _____ boxes

Solve the following problems.

1 Which of these rectangular prisms have a volume of 30 cubic units? Select the **three** correct answers.

A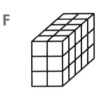

B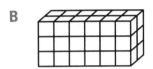

C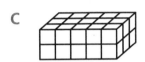

D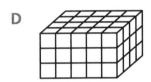

E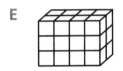

F

2 A rectangular prism that is 1 centimeter high has a volume of 56 cubic centimeters. If the prism is made up of 7 rows of 1-cubic-centimeter cubes, how many cubes are in each row?

Answer _____ cubes

3   Draw a model that can be used to find the volume of a figure with a length of 8 feet, a width of 1 foot, and a height of 3 feet.

4   Cassandra buys a wireless speaker like the one shown.

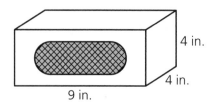

4 in.

4 in.

9 in.

Draw a model with unit cubes that can be used to find the volume of the speaker.

5 Giles is filling a rectangular swimming pool with water. A side of the pool is 20 feet long, another side is 10 feet long, and the depth of the pool is 4 feet.

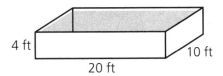

Explain how Giles can find the volume of the pool using a model and cubic units.

_____

_____

_____

6 Faith had 16 crates that measure 1 cubic foot each. She stacked them to form a rectangular prism.

Part A What was the volume of the prism Faith made with all the crates?

Answer _____ cubic feet

Part B Explain whether or not the figure below has the same volume as Faith's prism.

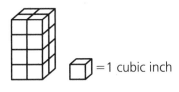

_____

_____

Part 1 Introduction

The area of a rectangle or square is found by multiplying the length and width. Area is the measurement of a flat or two-dimensional figure in square units. Find the volume of a rectangular prism or cube by using the three dimensions of the figure: length, width, and height.

> Volume = $l \times w \times h$
>
> or
>
> Volume = $B \times h$, where B is the area of the base

What is the volume of a stack of paper that is 2 inches high and made of sheets measuring 11 inches long by 8 inches wide?

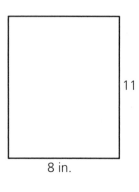

11 in.

8 in.

Find the area of one sheet of paper: 11 inches × 8 inches = 88 square inches.

A stack of paper has a height of 2 inches.

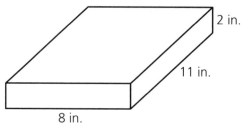

2 in.

11 in.

8 in.

Use the area of one sheet of paper times the height of the stack to find the volume of the stack.

$$V = l \times w \times h$$
$$V = 11 \times 8 \times 2 = 88 \times 2$$
$$V = 176 \text{ in.}^3$$

The volume of the stack of paper is 176 cubic inches.

> Volume is always given in cubic units.

Imagine modeling the stack of paper using unit cubes.

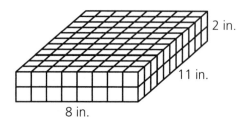

2 in.

11 in.

8 in.

There are 88 cubes on the top layer. The stack of paper has 2 layers of cubes with 88 cubes in each.

$$88 + 88 = 176$$

There are 176 cubes in the rectangular prism formed by the stack of papers.

The volume of the stack of cubes is 176 cubic inches, which is the same as the volume found by multiplying the dimensions of the stack of papers: $11 \times 8 \times 2 = 176$ cubic inches.

Think About It

Why is using the formula $V = B \times h$ the same as using the formula $V = l \times w \times h$?

_____

_____

Use the information given in diagrams and pictures to find the volume of figures.

➤ Minny collects old cameras. She has an old box camera like the one shown below.

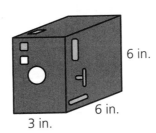

6 in.

6 in.

3 in.

What is the formula for the volume of a rectangular prism?

_____

What is the length of the camera? _____

What is the width of the camera? _____

What is the height of the camera? _____

Write an expression that can be used to find the volume of the box camera.

_____

What is the product of the length and width? _____

What part of the camera does this product represent?

_____

> The base of the camera is a rectangle.

What is the product of the length and the width and the height? _____

What is the volume of the box camera? _____

➤ A dollhouse is made up of a rectangular prism and a triangular prism, as shown below.

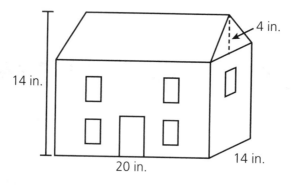

What is the length of the dollhouse? _____

What is the width of the dollhouse? _____

What is the total height of the dollhouse? _____

Can the total height be used in the volume formula to find the volume

of the rectangular prism? _____

> The total height of the dollhouse is the heights of the rectangular prism and the triangular prism.

How can you find the height of the rectangular prism portion of the house?

_____

What is the height of the rectangular prism? _____

What is the formula that can be used to find the volume of the rectangular

prism? _____

Write two expressions that can be used to find the volume of the rectangular prism.

_____

What is the volume of the rectangular prism portion of this dollhouse?

_____

Use what you know about volume to answer these questions.

1 What is the volume of the figure?

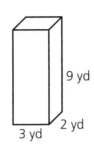

9 yd

3 yd 2 yd

_____

2 Write three multiplication expressions and an addition expression that can be used to find the volume of the figure.

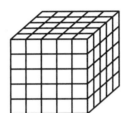

_____

Solve the following problems.

1 Armando bought the box of crackers shown below.

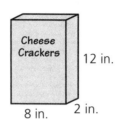

If the box were filled with 1-inch cubes, how many cubes would fit in the cracker box? Show your work.

> Find the area of the base first.

Answer _____ cubes

2 Jennifer ordered a new TV stand.

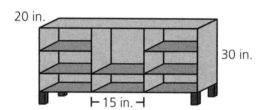

> The length of the stand is the total length of all of the shelves.

Each of the shelves has the same length and width. What is the volume of the TV stand? Explain how you found your answer.

_____

_____

_____

3 The associative property for multiplication is stated as $a \times (b \times c) = (a \times b) \times c$. Find the volume of a 3 in. by 4 in. by 5 in. rectangular prism using both sides of the equation. Show your work.

> Use the order of operations to simplify the terms in parentheses first.

Answer _____ cubic inches

Solve the following problems.

1   What is the volume of the rectangular prism? Show your work.

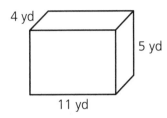

4 yd

5 yd

11 yd

Answer _____ cubic yards

2   Paige rents a moving truck with a cargo area measuring 12 feet long,
10 feet wide, and 9 feet tall. She needs exactly 1,000 cubic feet of space to
move all of her things. Which statement about the truck's volume is true?

A   It is 20 cubic feet less than Paige needs.

B   It is exactly 1,000 cubic feet.

C   It is 80 cubic feet more than Paige needs.

D   It is double the volume Paige needs.

Part 4

3 Tariq ships baseballs to sports equipment stores. Each baseball is in a box with a volume of 100 cubic inches. He ships the baseballs in one of the two crates below.

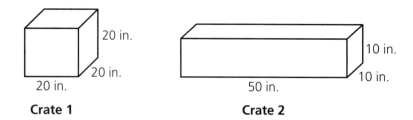

Crate 1　　　　　　**Crate 2**

Part A In which crate can Tariq ship more baseballs?

Answer _____

Part B The baseballs cost $0.50 each to ship. How much does it cost to ship the crate that fits the greatest number of baseballs? Explain.

_____

_____

_____

4 Boxed sets of DVDs of two different TV shows are shown.

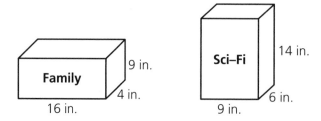

Choose an option from each set that makes the statement true.

The volume of the [family show,　sci-fi show] DVD set is [180,　576,　756] cubic inches greater than the volume of the other DVD set.

5 The box shown here was filled with 1-square centimeter sugar cubes. How many sugar cubes fit in the box?

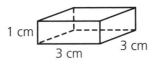

Answer _____ sugar cubes

6 The city science center has a leafcutter ant tank that has the dimensions shown.

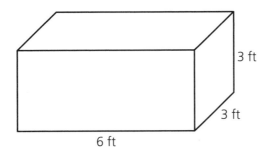

Part A   Draw a model that can be used to find the number of cubic feet that will fit into the tank, without calculating the volume.

Part B   What is the volume of the tank in cubic yards? Justify your answer using the model and volume formula.

_____

_____

_____

1 Introduction

Some figures are made of more than one rectangular prism. Find the volume of these irregular figures by finding the sum of the volumes of each part of the figure.

The diagram below shows a town library. What is the volume of the town library?

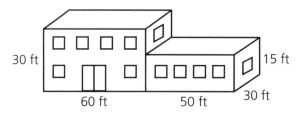

Find the volume of each part of the building. The left and right portions of the building have the same width of 30 feet.

The left part is 60 feet long, 30 feet wide, and 30 feet high. The volume of this part is $60 \times 30 \times 30 = 54{,}000$ cubic feet.

The right portion is 50 feet long, 30 feet wide, and 15 feet high. The volume of this part is $50 \times 30 \times 15 = 22{,}500$ cubic feet.

> Volume = *length* × *width* × *height*
>
> Volume = *Base* × *height*

Find the sum of the volumes: $54{,}000 + 22{,}500 = 76{,}500$ cubic feet

The volume of the library is 76,500 cubic feet.

Think About It

If you know the total volume of an irregular figure and the volume of part of the figure, how can you find the volume of the other part of the figure?

_____

_____

The volume of an irregular figure is made up of volumes of each part of the figure.

➤ Becky has the bookshelf shown in her bedroom.

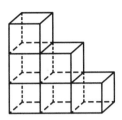

The shelf is made of a set of cubes with sides of 10 inches each. What is the total volume of the bookshelf?

What formula can be used to find the volume of each cube?

_____

What is the volume of each cube? _____

How many equally sized cubes are in the bookshelf? _____

Write an expression that can be used to find the volume of the bookshelf.

_____

What is the volume of the entire bookshelf? _____

> Volume is
> always
> measured in
> cubic units.

➤ Look at this figure.

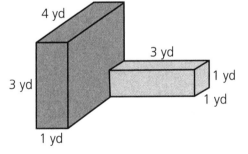

How many rectangular prisms make up this irregular figure? _____

What is the length of the dark green figure? _____ What is the

width? _____ What is the height? _____

> How can you
> break this figure
> into rectangular
> prisms?

What is the area of the base of the dark green figure? _____

Multiply the area of the base by the height to find the volume.

_____

What is the length of the light green figure? _____ What is the

width? _____ What is the height? _____

What is the volume of the light green figure? _____

How can you combine the volumes of these figures to find the volume of the

entire figure? _____

What is the volume of the irregular figure? _____

Use what you know about volume to answer these questions.

1 What is the volume of this figure?

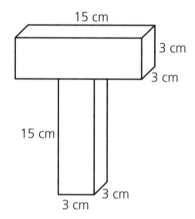

_____

2 The three parts of the figure are equal in size. What is the volume of the figure?

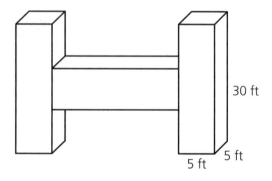

_____

Solve the following problems.

1 Paula made a custom cage for her rabbit. She attached a 2-ft by 3-ft by 3-ft cage to a larger cage that measures 4-ft by 4-ft by 3-ft. What is the volume of the custom cage?

> How many rectangular prisms make up this cage?

Answer _____ cubic feet

2 A real estate agent has this diagram of a house.

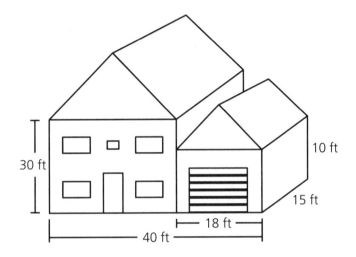

If the house and garage have the same depth, what is the volume of the rectangular portions of the house? Explain how you found your answer.

> How can you use the measurements that are given to find any missing measurements?

_____

_____

_____

_____

Solve the following problems.

1 Aidan and his dad plan to build the workshop shown here. It consists of a large studio and a small tool room. If they need at least 2,100 cubic feet for the workshop, will the workshop be big enough? Why, or why not?

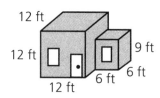

12 ft

12 ft   9 ft

12 ft   6 ft   6 ft

_____

_____

_____

2 A stage prop was made of two wooden boxes, each of which is a cube.

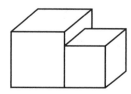

The height of the larger cube is 8 inches. The area of the base of the smaller cube is 36 square inches.

Part A What are the dimensions of each part of the prop?

_____

_____

Part B What is the total volume of the prop? Explain how you found your answer.

_____

_____

_____

_____

3 A Mayan pyramid is made of rectangular prisms. This model of a Mayan pyramid is in a gift shop.

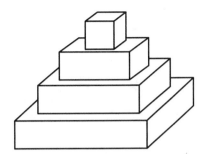

The bottom tier of the pyramid is a rectangular prism that is 4 inches long, 4 inches wide, and 1 inch high. If each tier is 1 inch high and has a length and width that is 1 inch shorter than the tier below it, what is the volume of the pyramid?

Answer _____ cubic inches

4 Mrs. Song is replacing the wooden steps leading to her house with steps made of concrete. The plans for the new steps are shown below.

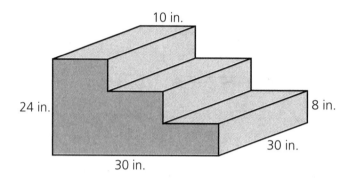

Part A Explain how to find the volume of the new steps.

_____

_____

_____

_____

Part B What volume of concrete will be used to make the steps? Show your work.

Answer _____ cubic inches

5 Ella has a birdhouse in her backyard like the one shown.

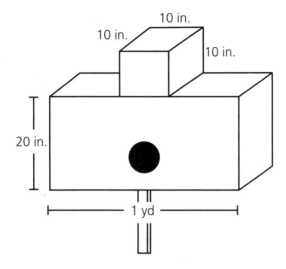

What is the volume of the birdhouse?

Answer _____ cubic inches

6 A small cube is stacked on top of a larger cube. The small cube has a side length of 5 yards. The large cube has a side length that is 2 yards longer than the small cube. What is the volume of the stacked cubes?

Answer _____ cubic yards

Solve the following problems.

1 This line plot shows the weights in ounces of some hamsters.

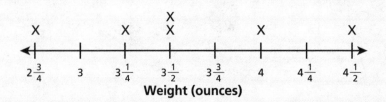

HAMSTERS

Weight (ounces)

How many hamsters weigh less than 4 ounces?

A one

B two

C four

D five

2 The countertop in a kitchen is 60 inches wide and 28 inches deep. What is the perimeter of the countertop in feet? Show your work.

Answer _____ feet

3 Rupert recorded these distances, in miles, that he biked daily.

$11\frac{1}{6}$ $10\frac{5}{6}$ $9\frac{3}{4}$ $10\frac{3}{6}$ $10\frac{2}{3}$ $10\frac{3}{4}$ $10\frac{5}{6}$ 11 $9\frac{5}{6}$ $10\frac{2}{3}$

Make a line plot for the data set below.

4 D'Nae is buying foam to fill a neck pillow. A 1-pound bag of foam costs $4.00. To buy less than 1 pound, D'Nae will spend $0.40 per ounce. D'Nae needs 14 ounces of foam.

Part A What is the cost per ounce of the 1-pound bag?

Answer $_____ per ounce

Part B Should D'Nae buy the foam by the ounce or by the pound to get the lowest price? Explain your answer.

_____

_____

5 What is the volume of the building shown below?

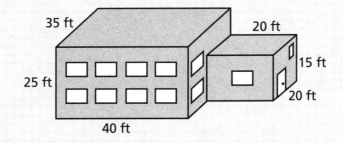

Answer _____ cubic feet

6 At a warehouse store, boxes are placed in large stacks in the aisles.

Part A A certain product is packed in a box that is 1 foot on each side. A stack of this product is 5 boxes long, 7 boxes wide, and 7 boxes high. What is the volume of this stack of boxes?

Answer _____ cubic feet

Part B Some pallets of boxes in one aisle of the warehouse store are shown below.

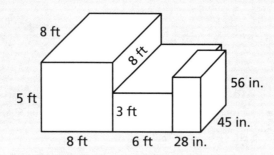

What is the total volume of these stacks, in cubic inches?

Answer _____ cubic inches

7 What is the volume of a rectangular prism with a length of 20 meters, a height of 18 meters, and a width of 2 meters?

Answer _____ cubic meters

8 Complete the table with the volume of each figure and the multiplication equation that shows the volume.

Figure	Volume (in cubic units)	Proof Using Multiplication

9 A company is sending 2,000 1-cubic yard boxes overseas in shipping containers. Each shipping container is 9 feet high, 9 feet wide, and 45 feet long.

Part A How many boxes can fit into one shipping container?

Answer _____ boxes

Part B How many shipping containers will the company need to ship all the boxes? How many boxes are packed in the last container? Show your work or explain how you found your answer.

_____

_____

_____

_____

10 Tanner is trying out a new recipe for soup.

Part A If he uses 6 cups of cream, 3 pints of broth, and 1 quart of water, will this make 1 gallon of soup? Explain.

_____

_____

Part B What unit should Tanner use to determine how many servings 1 gallon of soup will make? Explain.

_____

_____

_____

11 Len made this rectangular stack of 1-cubic yard boxes in a warehouse. How many boxes are in the stack?

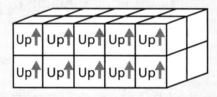

Answer _____ boxes

In grade 4, you learned about points, lines, and line segments, as well as classifying shapes. Now you can use what you know about points, coordinate planes, and polygons to locate points and solve problems using coordinate planes, and to classify figures.

LESSON 32 Using the Coordinate Plane In this lesson, you will locate points on a coordinate plane and draw conclusions based on the locations of points.

LESSON 33 Solving Problems with the Coordinate Plane In this lesson, you will solve real-world problems by using points on the first quadrant of a coordinate plane.

LESSON 34 Properties of Two-Dimensional Figures In this lesson, you will recognize the characteristics of polygons and congruent sides and angles.

LESSON 35 Classifying Two-Dimensional Figures In this lesson, you will classify figures based on their characteristics, such as their angles and sides.

1 Introduction

A **coordinate plane** is made of two number lines, or **axes.** One is horizontal and is called the **x-axis.** The other is vertical and is called the **y-axis.** The number lines intersect at the **origin,** or (0, 0).

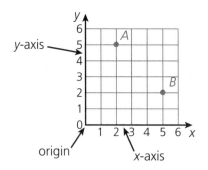

> *Vertical* means up and down. *Horizontal* means across.

Each point is described by an **ordered pair.** The coordinates in the ordered pair identify the location of the point on the coordinate plane. The **x-coordinate** is the first number. It tells the distance from 0, moving right. The **y-coordinate** is the second number. It tells the distance from 0, moving up.

> Ordered pairs are always in the same order.
> (x, y)

Look at point *A* on the coordinate plane above. Its ordered pair is (2, 5). Move 2 units right from 0. Then move 5 units up.

Look at point *B*. Its ordered pair is (5, 2). Move 5 units right from 0. Then move 2 units up.

Use an ordered pair to plot a point on a coordinate plane.

Plot a point at (4, 3) on the coordinate plane.

> The x-coordinate moves right.
> The y-coordinate moves up.

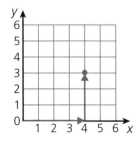

Look at the ordered pair (4, 3).

The x-coordinate is 4, so move 4 units to the right along the x-axis.

The y-coordinate is 3, so move 3 units up.

Think About It

Are the points at (2, 3) and (3, 2) at the same place on a coordinate plane? Explain how you know.

_____

_____

2 Focused Instruction

Sometimes ordered pairs are given in a table. The number in the *x*-column is the *x*-coordinate. The number beside it in the *y*-column is the *y*-coordinate. It may help you to rewrite them as an ordered pair.

➤ Peter graphs the points shown in the table on a coordinate plane.

x	y
0	3
1	4
2	5

Write the data from the table as a set of ordered pairs.

_____

In the first ordered pair, how far along the *x*-axis should Peter move for the *x*-coordinate?

_____

> Does the *x*-coordinate tell you to move up or to the right?

In the first ordered pair, how far along the *y*-axis should Peter move for the *y*-coordinate?

_____

Plot the point for (0, 3) on the coordinate plane below. Label it *A*.

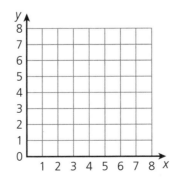

Look at point *A*. What do you think will always be true if the *x*-coordinate is 0?

_____

Explain how to graph the next two ordered pairs. Label them *B* and *C*.

_____

_____

_____

Graph the ordered pairs on the coordinate plane on page 267.

Connect the points. What kind of line do the points make?

_____

Points on a coordinate plane can be connected to form lines and shapes.

➤ The coordinate plane shows a square with points *A, B, C,* and *D*. What is the location of each point on the coordinate plane?

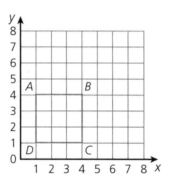

When graphing a point, in which direction do you move first?

_____

Which axis do you move along first when writing an ordered pair for a

point? _____

Ordered pairs:
(*x, y*)

From 0, how many units to the right should you move to get to point *A?*

_____

From the *x*-axis, how many units up should you move to get to point *A?*

_____

What is the ordered pair that describes the location of point *A?* _____

What is the ordered pair that describes the location of point *B?* _____

What is the ordered pair that describes the location of point *C?* _____

What is the ordered pair that describes the location of point *D?* _____

Use what you know about coordinate planes to find the ordered pairs that describes the points on the coordinate plane.

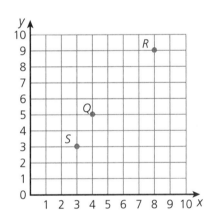

1 *Q* _____

2 *R* _____

3 *S* _____

Solve the following problems.

1 Which point is located at (9, 4)?

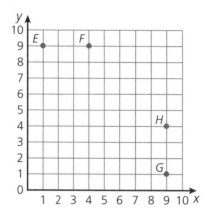

> Coordinate pairs are in the order of (x, y).

Answer _____

2 Describe how to graph a point at (5, 6) on a coordinate plane.

_____

_____

_____

> Which way do you move for the first number in an ordered pair?

3 On the coordinate plane below, draw a line segment with an endpoint M at (3, 5) and an endpoint N at (2, 1). Label each of the endpoints.

> A line segment is part of a line with two endpoints. It is straight.

Solve the following problems.

1 What is the location of the top point of the star?

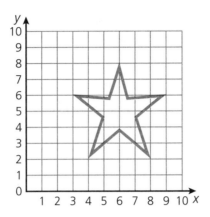

Answer _____

2 Use the coordinate plane to draw a line that passes through point *W* at (7, 0) and point *X* at (3, 4). Label each point.

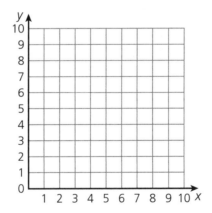

Use the coordinate plane below to answer problems 3–5.

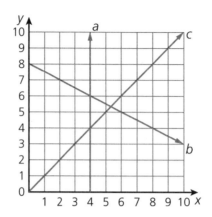

3 What ordered pair describes the location at which lines *a* and *b* meet?

Answer _____

4 Select an option in the set to make the following statement true.

For all the points on line *a*, the [*x*-coordinate,   *y*-coordinate] is always 4.

5 Explain how one line can be moved so that all three lines will meet at the same point.

_____

_____

6 The list below shows the ordered pairs for some points.

- *A* (2, 3)
- *B* (3, 2)
- *C* (3, 3)
- *D* (2, 2)
- *E* (3, 1)

Part A Graph the points from the list on the coordinate plane below.

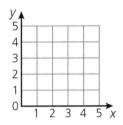

Part B A triangle is formed on the coordinate plane above. Its vertices are at (2, 1), (2, 4), and (4, 1). Which of the points that you graphed in Part A do not lie on one of the sides of this triangle? Explain your reasoning.

_____

_____

_____

1 Introduction

Coordinate planes can be used to solve problems, such as those involving distance and location. The scale on the axes can represent miles, feet, meters, or other measurement units.

A board game is arranged in a coordinate plane. Each player must predict the location of boats located on the plane. Some boats are placed on more than one point. Marilee predicts that there is a boat with an *x*-coordinate that is 3 units greater than a boat on (1, 4). Is she correct?

Look at the ordered pairs for the points with a boat:
(1, 4), (3, 2), (3, 3), (3, 1), (4, 1), and (5, 1).

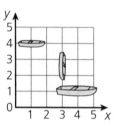

The *x*-coordinate of (1, 4) is 1.
Determine if one of the other points has an *x*-coordinate that is 3 units greater than 1.

The *x*-coordinate of (4, 1) is 3 units greater than the *x*-coordinate of (1, 4), because 1 + 3 = 4. So Marilee is correct.

Think About It

Name an example of something in your everyday life that could be plotted on a coordinate plane. Explain the points that are plotted and give an example of an ordered pair.

_____

_____

Coordinate planes can be used as maps. They can also be used to create geometric figures like triangles and rectangles.

➤ Gina used a coordinate plane to map the locations of her home, school, and the skate park. Each gridline represents a street. Each square on the plane represents one block. Gina only walks along two streets to get from home to school. How far does Gina walk to get to school each day?

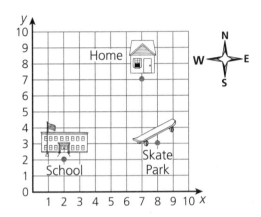

What is the location of Gina's home? _____

What is the location of the school? _____

If Gina walks south first, how many blocks will she walk in this direction?

_____

Which direction will Gina walk second? _____

How many blocks will Gina walk second? _____

If Gina walks west first, how many blocks will she walk in this direction?

_____

Which direction will Gina walk second? _____

How many blocks will Gina walk second? _____

Write an expression that can be used to find the total distance Gina walks, using

each direction as a separate addend. _____

What is the sum of the expression? _____

What is the total distance that Gina must walk to school?

_____

> Use the compass beside the map to find the directions.

➤ A rectangle has vertices *A* at (1, 1), *B* at (6, 1), and *C* at (1, 8). What is the location of the fourth vertex, point *D*?

> Ordered pair:
> (*x*, *y*)

What does the first number in an ordered pair show?

_____

What does the second number show?

_____

Locate and graph the locations of the three known vertices on the coordinate plane.

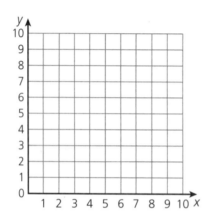

What is the length of side *AB*? _____

What is the length of side *AC*? _____

What is true about the lengths of the sides of a rectangle?

> A rectangle is a quadrilateral with four square corners. Opposite sides are parallel.

_____

What should the distance be between point *B* and the missing point *D*?

_____

What should the distance be between point *C* and the missing point *D*?

_____

What is the location of the missing vertex, point *D*? _____

Plot point *D* on the coordinate plane above. Complete the rectangle.

Is the difference between the *x*-coordinates of point *C* and point *D* equal to 5?

_____

Is the difference between the *y*-coordinates of point *B* and point *D* equal to 7?

_____

Use what you know about coordinate planes to answer these questions.

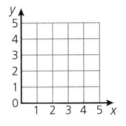

1 If a figure has vertices at (2, 2), (2, 4), and (5, 2), what is the figure?

_____

2 A library is located at (4, 1) and a swimming pool is located at (3, 2). The side of a square represents 1 mile and the gridlines represent streets. How far would it be to drive from the library to the swimming pool?

_____

Solve the following problems.

Use the coordinate plane below to answer problems 1 and 2.

The coordinate plane shows the location of wall murals in the downtown area of a city. The lines on the coordinate plane represent streets. The distance between the lines represent blocks.

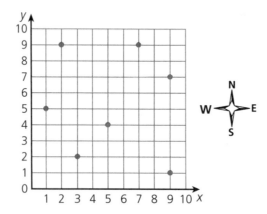

1 What is the distance between the wall murals with a *y*-coordinate of 9?

Answer _____ blocks

> Find the points with ordered pairs where $y = 9$.

2 A walking art tour starts at the mural at (3, 2) and then travels to another mural at (1, 5). The third stop on the tour is at (5, 4). How far did someone on the walking tour travel from the beginning of the tour to the third mural of the tour? Explain.

> Draw the routes between two points along the lines and count the sides of the squares.

_____

_____

_____

Solve the following problems.

The coordinate plane below shows the town of Smithville. Use the coordinate plane to answer problems 1 and 2.

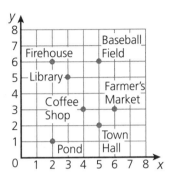

1 Lien, Etta, and May are meeting at the firehouse. Lien is coming from the pond. Etta is coming from the baseball field. May is coming from her house at (0, 6). Which girl will walk farthest?

    A   Lien

    B   Etta

    C   May

    D   They all walk the same distance.

2 To get home from the baseball field, Ian walks 4 units down and 2 units to the right. What are the coordinates of Ian's house?

    Answer _____

3 Brett drew a square with an area of 25 square units on the coordinate plane. The first vertex of the square is located at (1, 3). Draw Brett's square on the coordinate plane below.

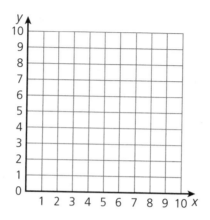

Use the coordinate plane below to answer problems 4 and 5.

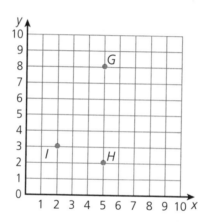

4 If point *I* is moved so that the *y*-coordinate is decreased by 1, what type of triangle is created by connecting the points?

Answer _____

5 A fourth point is added to the coordinate plane. If the ordered pair for *G* is (*x*, *y*), then the new point is located at (*x* − 3, *y* − 1). What is the location of the fourth point?

Answer _____

6 Ed wants to plant pepper plants in a section of his garden. He starts to mark off the section at one corner, point *A*. He marks the next corner 4 units up at point *B*. He walks 6 units to the right of point *B* and marks the third corner at point *C*. Then he walks 4 units down to point *D* to mark the fourth corner.

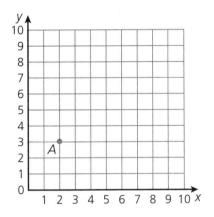

Part A What are the coordinates of points *A*, *B*, *C*, and *D*?

Point *A* _____

Point *B* _____

Point *C* _____

Point *D* _____

Part B Ed decides to grow two different kinds of peppers and wants to split his pepper section in half. Between what two points could he draw a line to divide this section in half? Explain your answer.

_____

_____

_____

_____

CCSS: 5.G.3

Properties of Two-Dimensional Figures

1 Introduction

Two-dimensional figures, or plane figures, have two dimensions: length and width. Some plane figures have straight sides and angles. These figures are called **polygons.** Polygons can be identified by their attributes, including types of angles and characteristics of sides.

Triangles	Quadrilaterals	Other Polygons	Circles
• 3 sides • angles have a sum of 180°	• 4 sides • angles have a sum of 360°	• more than 4 sides • angle sum is greater than 360°	• closed curve • interior angle measures 360°

There are many different kinds of plane figures that fit within the categories in the chart.

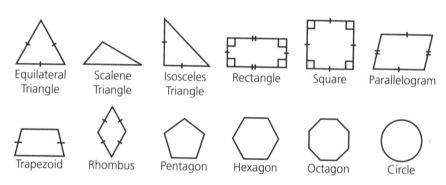

Equilateral Triangle　Scalene Triangle　Isosceles Triangle　Rectangle　Square　Parallelogram

Trapezoid　Rhombus　Pentagon　Hexagon　Octagon　Circle

> A triangle with one right angle is a **right triangle.**
>
> A triangle with one obtuse angle is an **obtuse triangle.**
>
> A triangle with three acute angles is an **acute triangle.**

Figures can also be described by the measure of their angles. **Acute angles** measure less than 90°. **Right angles** measure exactly 90°. **Obtuse angles** measure greater than 90°. Figures with right angles are marked with squares in the corner to show the right angle.

The angles opposite congruent sides are congruent angles, or angles that have the same measurement. They are often marked with curved lines with tick marks to show that they are equal.

> **Congruent** means "equal in size." Congruent sides and angles are marked with tick marks.

Figures can be named based on their properties.

This triangle is a scalene triangle because its sides are all different lengths. It is also a right triangle because it has one right angle.

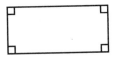

This quadrilateral is a parallelogram because it has two pairs of parallel sides. It is also a rectangle because it has four right angles.

Think About It

Describe an object or a place in real life that is a parallelogram. Explain what makes it a parallelogram.

_____

_____

2 Focused Instruction

Triangles can be named based on their sides and based on their angles.

➤ A triangle has sides of 3 inches, 3 inches, and 4.24 inches. It also has two congruent angles. What is true about this type of triangle?

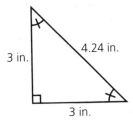

3 in.

4.24 in.

3 in.

What are the side lengths of the triangle?

_____

Are any of the sides lengths equal? _____

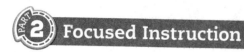

How many of the side lengths are equal? _____

What type of triangle has this many congruent sides?

_____

How many congruent angles does the triangle have?

_____

Using the picture, how can you tell the angles are congruent?

_____

Can you tell if any of the angles are congruent if you only know the lengths of the sides? Explain.

_____

What type of angle is the third angle in this triangle? _____

What type of name can you give this triangle based on the sides?

_____

What type of name can you give this triangle based on the angles?

_____

What symbol on a picture shows that things are congruent?

There are many different types of quadrilaterals. All quadrilaterals have certain properties, even if they look different from one another.

➤ Look at the figures below.

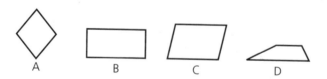

How many sides do each of the figures above have? _____

What is the name for figures with this number of sides?

_____

What type of angles does figure B have? _____

How many angles does figure B have? _____

Figure B has square corners.

What is the sum of the measures of the angles in figure B? _____

In figure A, two angles measure 50° and two angles measure 130°. What is the

sum of the measures of the angles in figure A? _____

In figure D, the angles measure 30°, 60°, 120°, and 150°. What is the sum of the

measures of the angles in figure D? _____

What do you think the sum of the angles in figure C is? _____

Explain why you think this.

_____

Use what you know about polygons to answer these questions.

1   Which of the triangles are scalene and right?

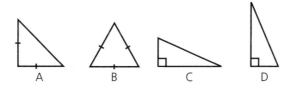

_____

2   In the space below, draw a figure with an angle sum of 360°.

Solve the following problems.

1 Toshiro measures the angles of a triangle and finds they are all different. What else must be true about this triangle?

> An angle has a relationship with the side that it is across from.

Answer _____

2 A game show has clues that players must figure out. One of the clues read on the show is shown below.

> What figure has only two parallel sides?

> I have only one pair of parallel sides.
>
> I also have one pair of congruent sides.
>
> What am I?

Draw and name the figure described by the clue.

Answer _____

3 Kevin explains that the figures shown on the geoboards do not have the same name.

> Look at the side lengths of each figure.

Is Kevin correct? Explain.

_____

_____

Solve the following problems.

1 A triangle has two congruent sides. The angle opposite one of the congruent sides measures 50°. What is the measure of the angle opposite the other congruent side?

    A 50°

    B 80°

    C 100°

    D 130°

2 An acute triangle is always an isosceles triangle. Is this statement true? Explain how you know.

_____

_____

_____

3 At the beginning of a game of pool, the balls are organized into a triangle using a tool called a rack. What kind of triangle is the rack shown here?

    Answer _____

4 Which statement correctly describes rectangles and squares? Select the **two** correct answers.

    A   A rectangle is a square, because it has 4 right angles.

    B   A rectangle is a square, because it has 2 pairs of parallel sides.

    C   A square is a rectangle, because it has 2 pairs of parallel sides.

    D   A rectangle is a square, because it has 2 pairs of parallel and congruent sides.

    E   A square is a rectangle, because it has 2 pairs of parallel sides and 4 right angles.

    F   A square and a rectangle are both parallelograms because they have 2 pairs of congruent sides.

    G   A square and a rectangle are both parallelograms because they have 2 pairs of parallel sides.

5 A kite has 2 pairs of congruent non-parallel sides. It also has 2 obtuse angles and 2 acute angles. Is the kite considered a parallelogram or a quadrilateral? Explain.

_____

_____

6   Rihana is working on a project for an art class. She starts with a square sheet of paper. Then she draws lines to divide the paper into different sections. She will paint each quadrilateral a different color. Her project is shown below, after she has drawn the lines.

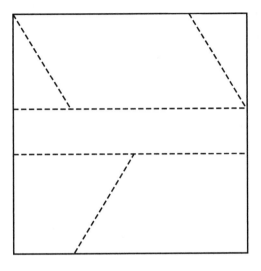

Part A   How many quadrilaterals did Rihana make with the lines she drew? Number the quadrilaterals in the diagram above. What are they?

_____

_____

Part B   Are all the types of quadrilaterals represented in Rihana's art project? Explain your answer.

_____

_____

_____

_____

7 Scott drew the two figures described below.

- Figure 1 has an angle sum of 180° and congruent sides.

- Figure 2 has one more side than a figure with an angle sum of 180°. It has non-right angles and more than one pair of parallel sides.

Draw and label Scott's figures in the space below.

Classifying Two-Dimensional Figures

1 Introduction

Two-dimensional figures can be classified into groups based on their characteristics, such as angles, parallel sides, and congruent sides.

This table shows you how to classify a triangle.

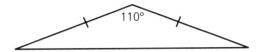

TRIANGLES

By Angles			By Sides		
Acute	**Obtuse**	**Right**	**Equilateral**	**Isosceles**	**Scalene**
3 angles that are less than 90° each	1 angle that is greater than 90°	1 angle that is equal to 90°	3 sides of equal length	at least 2 sides of equal length	no sides of equal length

Identifying both the angle and side attributes can help you classify triangles.

The triangle has 2 equal sides and an angle greater than 90°. Having 2 equal sides means the triangle is an isosceles triangle. The angle greater than 90° means that the triangle is obtuse.

> Sides marked with tick marks are congruent.

110°

This is both an isosceles and an obtuse triangle.

This chart shows you how to classify quadrilaterals.

All of the figures in the chart are quadrilaterals. A square is a type of rectangle and rhombus. The square, rectangle, and rhombus are parallelograms.

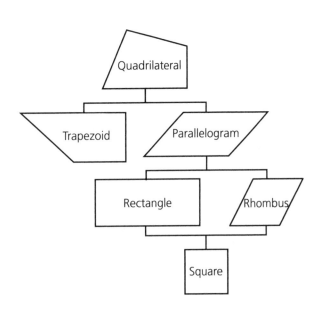

Think About It

A polygon is a closed figure with sides that are line segments. Is a circle considered a polygon and a plane figure? Explain.

_____

_____

Classify triangles based on their angles and their side lengths.

➤ Jeff's backyard has a triangular shape and is bordered by the house and two sides of fencing.

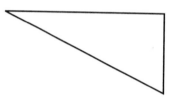

He knows that the angle created by the two fences measures 90°. He also knows that the shortest side is about 12 feet. The longest side is about 25 feet. The remaining side is 10 feet greater than the shortest side. Classify the yard shape using both the angles and side lengths.

What is the measure of the known angle of the backyard? _____

What is the name for an angle of this measure?

```
A right angle
makes a square
corner.
```

_____

What is the measure of the longest side? _____

What is the measure of the shortest side? _____

How can you find the measure of the remaining side?

_____

What is the measure of the remaining side? _____

Are any of the sides equal? _____

What type of triangle has sides with this relationship?

_____

What are the angle and side classifications for this triangle?

_____

What type of triangle is Jeff's backyard? _____

Classify quadrilaterals based on parallel and congruent sides and the number of right angles.

➤ A scouting group has a troop flag shaped like the one below.

The top of the flag is parallel to the bottom of the flag. The middle line of the flag is parallel to the bottom of the flag. Classify the green section of the flag.

Are the top and bottom of the flag parallel? _____

Are the bottom of the flag and the middle line parallel? _____

Are the middle line and top of the flag parallel? _____

How do you know?

_____

_____

Are the right and left sides of each section parallel? _____

What type of figure has these types of sides? _____

How many sides does the green section of the flag have? _____

What larger group does this figure fit within?

_____

Parallel lines never meet. They are always the same distance apart.

Is the figure in all of the same classifications as a rectangle? Why or why not?

_____

_____

Use what you know about two-dimensional figures to answer these questions.

1 Which of the figures is not a parallelogram?

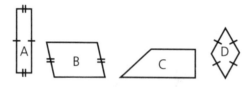

_____

2 Which of the figures is an acute isosceles triangle?

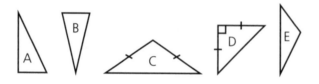

_____

Solve the following problems.

1 Mr. Delgado uses the ladder shown to hang pictures. What kind of triangle is formed by the sides of the ladder and the ground?

> First, look at the triangle's angles. Then look at its sides.

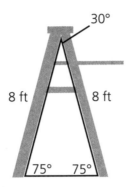

30°

8 ft   8 ft

75°   75°

Answer _____

2 Look at the figure below.

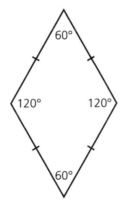

60°

120°   120°

60°

> How many right angles are in the figure?

Use the angles to determine what type of figure it is.

Answer _____

3 Irina classified a rectangle as a parallelogram. Is she correct? Explain.

> What makes a figure a parallelogram? Is this true for a rectangle?

_____

_____

_____

_____

Solve the following problems.

1   A triangle has sides that are 16 feet, 16 feet, and 16 feet in length. One angle is 60°. Which choice best describes the triangle?

   A   right and isosceles

   B   obtuse and scalene

   C   acute and isosceles

   D   acute and equilateral

2   A four-sided figure with two right angles has two additional angles that are congruent to each other. The figure also has sides that are congruent.

   Part A   What is the measure of the two remaining angles? Explain how you found your answer.

   _____

   _____

   Part B   What are all of the classifications for this figure?

   Answer _____

3 A typical baseball field is shown below. The right angle symbols mark the locations of first base, second base, third base, and home plate.

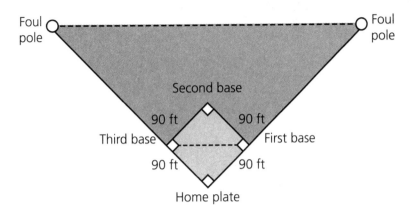

Part A During practice, the coach has the players throw the ball from first to second base, from second to third base, and from third base back to first base. What kind of triangle does the path of the ball make? Explain your answer.

_____

_____

_____

Part B The first and third baselines extend into the outfield and end at the foul poles. The left field foul pole is 318 feet from home plate. The right field foul pole is 314 feet from home plate. Is the triangle formed by the first and third base lines and the dashed line between them the same as the triangle formed in Part A? Explain your answer.

_____

_____

_____

4 Sen-Yung is flying her kite at the park. The outside edges of the green section of the kite are congruent. The outside edges of the gray section of the kite are congruent. There are no pairs of sides that are parallel.

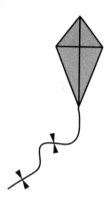

Which classification group does the kite fit within?

Answer _____

5 A typical football field is shown here.

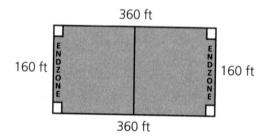

What is the most specific description of the shape of the football field?

Answer _____

6 Mark the correct space in the table to show the classifications for each polygon. You may mark more than one space for some polygons.

	Square	Rectangle	Rhombus	Parallelogram	Other Quadrilateral
□					
⬜ (trapezoid)					
▭					
◇					
▱					

Solve the following problems.

1   Jessica's house is at (2, 4). She walks up 3 units and right 3 units to take her dog to the park. From there, she walks right 3 units and down 3 units to the pet store to buy her dog a bone.

Part A   On the coordinate plane, mark the locations of Jessica's house, the park, and the pet store. Label each place with its name and coordinates.

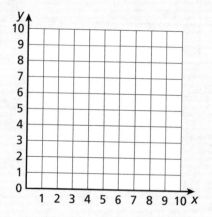

Part B   After visiting the pet store, Jessica returns home. If she were to ignore the grid lines and walk directly to each stop, what figure would her path form? Explain your answer.

_____

_____

2   Mark True or False for each of the following statements.

	True	False
A square is a type of rhombus.	☐	☐
A trapezoid is a type of parallelogram.	☐	☐
A triangle with acute angles can sometimes be an equilateral triangle.	☐	☐

3 Write a set of directions for graphing the ordered pair (5, 9).

_____

_____

4 A quadrilateral has two sides that measure 14 centimeters each and two sides that measure 5 centimeters each. Two angles measure 110° each, and the other two angles measure 70° each. The congruent angles are opposite, and the congruent sides are parallel. What kind of quadrilateral is it?

A   square

B   trapezoid

C   rectangle

D   parallelogram

5 The coordinate plane shows the locations of each student table in a classroom.

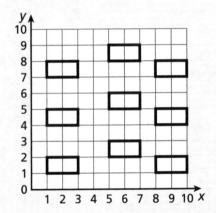

Stefan sits at a table with a corner at (8, 2). Stefan moves to a table that has a corner 3 units left and 6 units up. Circle the table where Stefan now sits.

6 Harrison draws a plane figure with two parallel sides that are 17 centimeters long each and two parallel sides that are 23 centimeters long each. All sides meet at right angles.

Part A What are the names Harrison could use to describe his figure?

Answer _____

Part B Harrison draws a line between two opposite corners of his figure and cuts the figure in half. Describe the two congruent figures he creates. Explain your answer.

_____

_____

_____

_____

7 A map has a shopping mall located at the point (1, 10). There is a city park located at (7, 6).

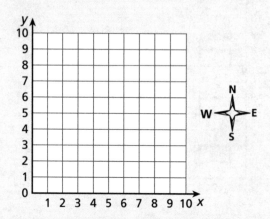

If each unit equals 1 mile, describe how the x- and y-coordinates change. Then give directions for driving to the park from the mall. The directions on the map move according to the compass rose shown.

_____

_____

_____

8 Freddie drew a triangle that has an angle measuring 105°. Which of these terms could describe Freddie's triangle? Select the **three** correct answers.

A acute

B scalene

C right

D equilateral

E isosceles

F obtuse

9 Look at the coordinate plane shown.

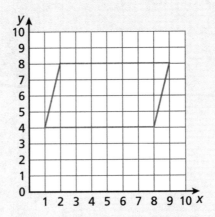

Amos drew a line from (2, 4) to (2, 8) and another line from (8, 4) to (8, 8) to make a new figure. Can the new figure be classified in the same group as the original figure? Explain your answer.

_____

_____

_____

GLOSSARY

A

acute angle: an angle that measures less than 90°

acute triangle: a triangle with three acute angles

area model: a way of showing multiplication using a rectangle divided into rows and columns of squares

array: a model using rows and columns of symbols or shapes

axes: the number lines used in a coordinate plane

B

base: the number that is multiplied by itself in an exponential expression; example: in 10^2, the number 10 is the base

C

common denominator: a number that is a multiple of every denominator of the fractions in a set

congruent: equal in length, measure, or shape

conversion factor: a number used to change units from one kind to another

coordinate plane: the space defined by two number lines placed at right angles and used to locate points in space in relation to their distances from the number lines

cubic unit: the amount of space inside a cube that measures 1 unit on each edge

customary system: a system of measurement used in the United States. It includes units of

- length—inch, foot, yard, mile
- capacity—fluid ounce, cup, pint, quart, gallon
- weight—ounce, pound, ton

D

data: information

decimals: numbers with values in places to the right of the decimal point

denominator: the number of parts in the whole or set, the number on the bottom of a fraction

dividend: the number being divided in a division problem

divisor: the number doing the dividing in a division problem

E

equals sign: the symbol =; means the expressions on each side have the same value

equation: a number sentence that says two expressions are equal

equilateral triangle: a triangle with three sides of the same length and three 60° angles

equivalent fractions: two or more fractions that represent the same value

expanded form: a way to write a number in which each digit is expressed as the product of its face value and a power of ten

exponent: the number that tells how many times another number (the base) is used as a factor; example: in 10^2, the 2 is the exponent

expression: a grouping of numbers and operations that shows the value of something

evaluate: to find the value of an expression

F

factors: whole numbers that multiply to form a product

G

greater than sign: the symbol >; means the expression on the left has a greater value than the expression on the right

I

improper fraction: a fraction in which the numerator is equal to or greater than the denominator

input: in a set of two variables, the value that the rule is applied to

input-output table: a table that shows two sets of values that are related by a rule

inverse operations: operations that undo each other, opposite operations. Addition and subtraction are inverse operations. Multiplication and division are inverse operations.

isosceles triangle: a triangle with at least two equal sides

L

leading zero: a zero in the ones place of a decimal number

least common denominator: the least common multiple shared by two denominators

less than sign: the symbol <; means the expression on the left has a smaller value than the expression on the right

line plot: a plot in which data is represented by Xs placed over a number line; also called a dot plot

lowest terms: a fraction in which the terms cannot be divided by a number other than 1; simplest form

M

metric system: a system of measurement used in most of the world. It includes units of

- length—millimeter, centimeter, meter, kilometer
- capacity—milliliter, liter
- mass—gram, kilogram

mixed number: a whole number plus a fraction

N

numerator: the number of parts talked about, the number on the top of a fraction

O

obtuse angle: an angle that measures more than 90° but less than 180°

obtuse triangle: a triangle with one obtuse angle

order of operations: the order in which operations are performed in a multi-operation expression: parentheses, exponents, multiplication and division from left to right, addition and subtraction from left to right

ordered pair: two numbers that name the location of a point on a coordinate plane; (x, y)

origin: the center of a coordinate plane, located at the intersection of the x- and y-axes, having the coordinates $(0, 0)$

output: in a set of two variables, the value that results from the rule of the pattern

P

pattern: a series of numbers that follow a given rule

place value: the value given to the place a digit has in a number; each place has a value 10 times greater than the place to its right.

Hundred Billions	Ten Billions	Billions	Hundred Millions	Ten Millions	Millions	Hundred Thousands	Ten Thousands	Thousands	Hundreds	Tens	Ones	Tenths	Hundredths	Thousandths
1	2	3,	4	5	6,	7	8	9,	0	1	2	.3	4	5

polygon: a two-dimensional figure with line segments for sides

power: the product of multiplying a number by itself

product: the answer in a multiplication problem

Q

quotient: the answer in a division problem

R

reciprocal: the number that multiplies another number for a product of 1

right angle: an angle that measures 90°

right triangle: a triangle with one right angle

rounding: to replace a number with a number that tells about how many or how much

S

scale: to resize a number by multiplying by a factor greater than, equal to, or less than 1

scalene triangle: a triangle with no equal sides

standard form: a number written as the sum of the values of its places

T

trailing zero: a 0 at the right end of a decimal number

U

unit cube: a cube that measures 1 unit wide, 1 unit long, and 1 unit high

V

volume: the amount of space inside an object

x-axis: the horizontal axis of a coordinate plane

x-coordinate: the first number in an ordered pair, it names the horizontal position of a point

y-axis: the vertical axis of a coordinate plane

y-coordinate: the second number in an ordered pair, it names the vertical position of a point

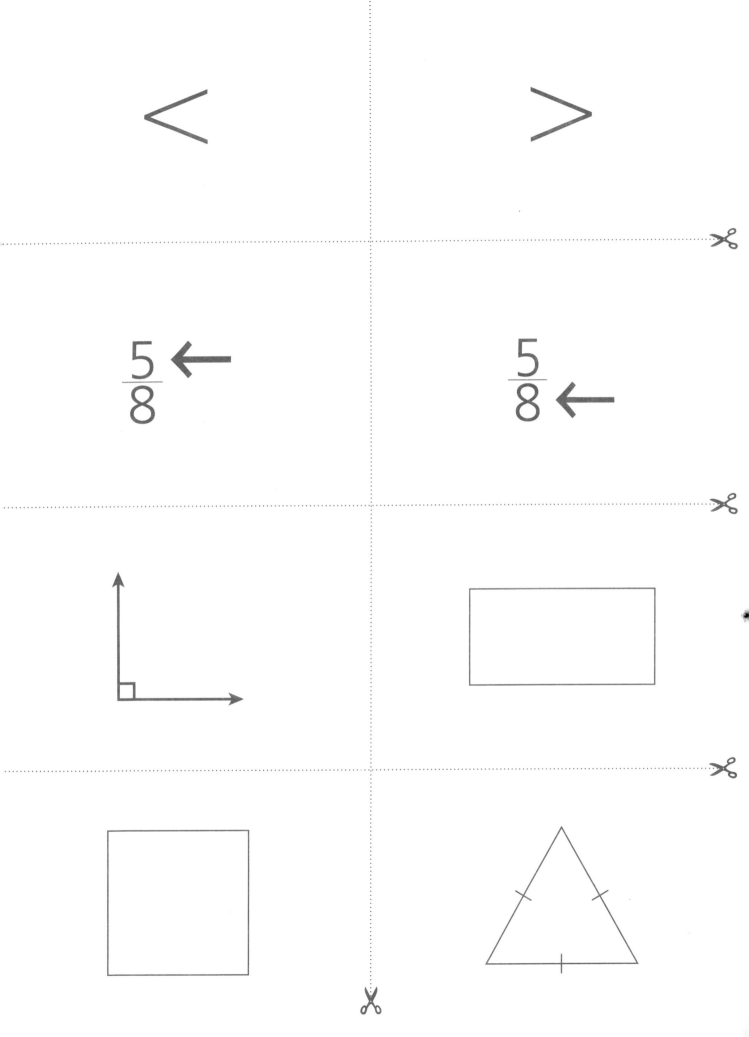

is greater than symbol	is less than symbol
denominator	numerator
rectangle	right angle
equilateral triangle	square

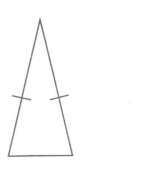

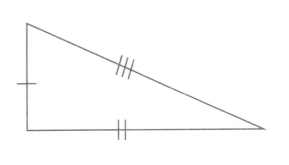

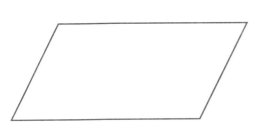

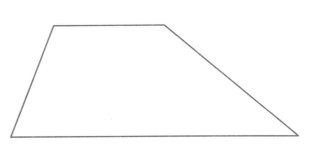

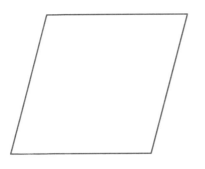

$$A = lw$$

$$V = lwh$$

number of inches
in a foot

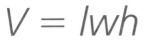

scalene triangle

isosceles triangle

trapezoid

parallelogram

area of a rectangle

Area = length × width

rhombus

volume of a rectangular prism

Volume =
length × width × height

12

number of feet
in a yard

number of hours
in a day

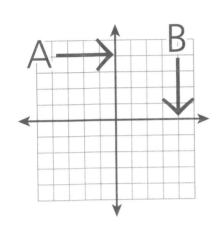

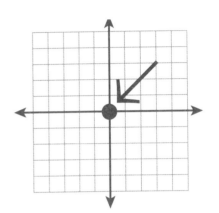

(4, 2)
↑

number of
milligrams
in a gram

number of
millimeters
in a meter

(4, 2)
↑

24

3

origin (0, 0)

A: *y*-axis
B: *x*-axis

1,000

y-coordinate

x-coordinate

1,000

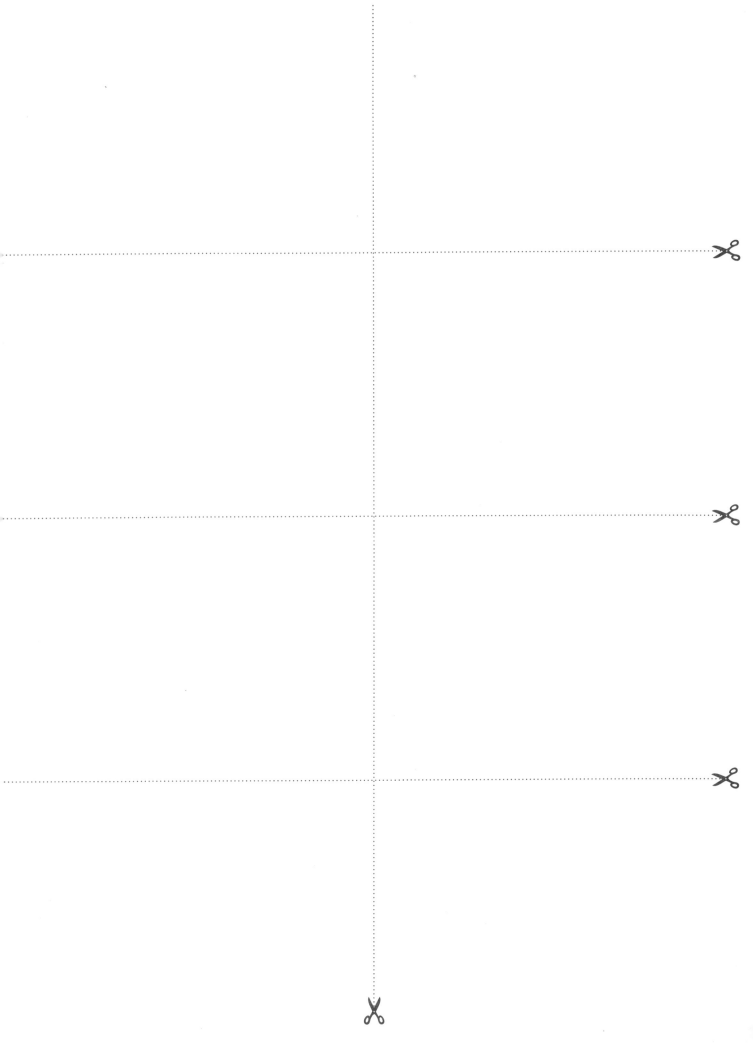